Transforming Economy

Transforming Economy

From Corrupted Capitalism
to Connected Communities

Zeus Yiamouyiannis, Ph.D.

Cover design and typesetting by Janet Brent.

ISBN-10: 0615838707

ISBN-13: 978-0615838700

TABLE OF CONTENTS

Part III - Connected Communities: Embracing the Future of Democratic Capitalism

ACKNOWLEDGMENTS

My deepest thanks go to Charles Hugh Smith. His support, collegiality, and thoughtful commentary both prompted and immensely improved this book. Our friendship and commitment to a healthy, creative, practical economics alternative inspired me to write for a public audience. This book is based on my guest posts for Charles's blog OfTwoMinds.com where they enjoyed a wide audience and were re-posted to other popular websites like ZeroHedge.com. Charles also introduced me to Dennis Fetcho, Stacy Herbert and Max Keiser, whom I must also thank for having me on their radio and television programs. I am grateful also to Geoffrey Gaskins for his spiritual insight, business acumen, and technical help in preparing a launch for this book. To my family, my wife Kelly, and son, Phoenix, thanks for your patience and inspiration to finish. Thanks to Peter Barnes and Mesa Refuge for giving me the seed to "write on the edge" of the human economy. Special thanks to Jona Kessans and Janet Brent for their professional collaboration and spiritual partnership in getting this book ready for the public. To my friends, blessings on your support and excitement over seeing this book published. To the truth-speaking community of alternative economics bloggers, analysts, and futurists, I deeply appreciate and benefit from your incisive research and investigation. Keep the faith. To my fellow world citizens, connecting across political, economic, and national backgrounds in alliance for a truly democratic capitalism, may this book provide one more brick to the construction of a new home for value and character.

INTRODUCTION

"We are the Change We Wish to See"

W hy do we resist change? Even when our very lives depend upon it, we find ourselves refusing to absorb the full truth of our present human situation. Is it too much for us? Do we really understand what change can be?

Here is what I believe is going on: We have been taught, often with ulterior motives, to understand change as something that happens *to us*, as something beyond our control. In this framework, you and I logically avoid change. If we can't do anything about change, why waste our time?

But what if change is something that happens *from us*, something we choose, initiate, and develop? What if refusing to initiate and participate in constructive, personal and collaborative change is tantamount to signing a death warrant for future generations?

We live in just such an unprecedented time, where our past decisions now threaten the very life of the planet we live on— global warming, polluted rivers, unsustainable economies, bought and paid-for politicians, obsolete education have consolidated into an undeniable reality: Things cannot go on as before. We know we will change.

The only issues are whether change will be done to us or proceed from us. We can be swept up by change as with a raging flood, or we can choose change and "learn to transform."

This book and its associated website, Citizen Zeus (http://citizenzeus. com), operate on a premise of democratic, creative change, that we can learn the craft of conscious transformation in order to meet the exciting and daunting challenges of our times.

In order to do this effectively this book will help you:

- Awaken to your present condition. Understand *what* is going on economically.

- Unleash possibilities for the future. Discuss *how* to move forward.

- Connect to a growing, healthy body of change, and understand *why*.

We humans are built for change. We may be the most adaptable organisms on the planet. It's time we embrace, rather than resist, our greatest ability.

READING AND USING THIS BOOK WITH AN EYE TOWARD TRANSFORMATION

This book shares new thinking and practices to transform obsolete economic commitments and beliefs. The writing is meant to be compelling, informative, and interesting, but even more it intends to help you apply new economic understanding to how you make family and community choices and how you live our individual life.

It is more important for me, as an author and activist, for you to maximize your use of the book and your time, so I will lay out a map and leave it up to you to pick the materials that will allow you to get the most out of this book.

Transforming Economy is divided up into three basic parts, "Corrupted Capitalism," "Transforming Economy," and "Connected Communities." If you are deeply interested in economic intrigue, I suggest you start at the beginning. If you are more interested in what is going on now so you can manage your choices and investments, you may want to start in the second section. If you are a person interested in future change and your time is limited, feel free to skip to Part III. Part III has a good summary and review of previous parts, and it goes right to the "juice" of what alternatives we can pursue on a personal, community, and international level.

My hope is that, no matter where you start, you will find a reason to come back and delve further into the book and the troubled but fascinating system it describes.

We can have a bright future if we get real with the current nature of our economic system, if we make sound, courageous choices, and if we invent our way forward.

I. Corrupted Capitalism: Learning from the Past—
This is a no-holds-barred exposé of the rampant, unapologetic fraud of our global financial system. This section gives notions like "debts are assets" an analytical thrashing. It is a readable, but sometimes detailed, examination of the "way things work now" as the culmination of a series of ill-fated past choices. It explores the irrationality of our present system, but also offers practical policy directions to help mitigate the effects of that irrationality, and it points to a way out of our present predicament. If you are more interested in the policy alternatives, and less in the current economic specifics please feel free to skim over the more detailed explanation and spend more time with the personal and policy alternatives at the end of each chapter.

Chapter 1: Imaginary Worth, Empire of Debt: How Modern Finance Created Its Own Downfall.

Chapter 2: Unhinged: When Concrete Reality No Longer Matters to the Market (and What to Do About It)

Chapter 3: Fighting and Winning When The Market has Cancer: How Unregulated Profit Cannibalizes the Economic Body and How Democratic Citizens Can Effectively Respond

II. Transforming Economy: Understanding the Present Challenges and Opportunities— This is the fulcrum section of the book. This section describes where we are now, caught as we are in that uncomfortable place between old economic momentum and new realities. In this transition, knowledge is power, if we can emotionally face what knowledge reveals. What is happening socially and economically? What are the effects and investment implications likely to be? How will the current trends play out? This middle stage can look depressing, so it requires a certain degree of tough-mindedness. Fraud has spread, created real suffering, and appears to have the upper hand, but, as I describe, fraud will break down amid the reality of math and the choices of world citizens to resist, withdraw support, and organize proactively.

Chapter 4: The Big Squeeze: Predicting the Effects of Savings Extortion and Abuse of the Middle Class

Chapter 5: Endgame: When Debt is Fraud, Debt Forgiveness is the Last and Only Remedy

Chapter 6: Money from Nothing: A Primer on Fake Wealth Creation and its Implications

Chapter 7: The First Dominoes: Greece, Reality, and Cascading Default

III. Connected Communities: Embracing the Future of Democratic Capitalism— This section addresses the strong, pragmatic, and hopeful alternatives to our present system. The most important quotes and elements of the previous sections are combined with a discussion of emerging technological and social innovation in order to create a new way forward. This section is how the story can turn out if we apply human creativity, integrity, and productivity. This is how the story can turn out if we respect, develop, and link each other's deeper contributions.

Chapter 8: Making a Living vs. Making a Killing: Creating a Healthy Democratic Foundation for Economies

Chapter 9: Unleashing the Future: Advancing Prosperity Through Debt Forgiveness

Chapter 10: "I Give A Damn": A Capitalist Manifesto for the Productive Class

Chapter 11: Youth of the World Unite!: How Younger Generations Can Lead the Way To a New Frontier

The greatest mistake

> The dollar is something like an inch (not wealth but a measure of wealth)... People think money has to come from somewhere like hydroelectric power or lumber or iron, and it doesn't. Money is something we invent."
> – Alan Watts
> (http://karmajello.com/universe/knowledge/alan-watts-money-non-sense.html)

Perhaps the greatest human error we make is mistaking measurement of value (i.e. money) for value itself. Almost every economic sin, every fraud, can be traced to this critical point. Measurement can be invented out of thin air, but value must be produced either by blood, sweat, and tears or by some other means.

Money has no inherent value. It is a measurement of value. If money does not represent substantial value, it is worthless. Our current global monetary system is a "fiat" system, where measurement-money, backed by nothing is applied to things, i.e. debt, that are simply more valueless measurement. There is no "there" there.

In the big picture, money's real asset power lies in its ability to facilitate exchange and circulation of human effort, productivity, and creativity. A mere printed dollar has no real asset value.

Empty money + greed = corrupted economy

Our tough choices now mean that we are coming to terms with our worship of empty money, which cannibalizes value rather than adds value and which enables exploitation rather than production.

If we allow this to go on, if we continue worshipping money without value, we will possess no value. We will have surrendered ourselves to a phantom. Combine this with rampant greed and you have a corrupted economy. Greed, as I define it, is worship of valueless money combined with a desire for wealth without effort.

When the Bible says, "The love of money (greed) is the root of all evil (1 Timothy 6:10), it is not making primarily a moral statement. It is making a practical statement. Our own economic system has proven the disastrous working consequences of greed, especially when combined with the effort to make mere measurement-money equate with value.

The only thing that keeps an economy afloat is the value and effort we bring to it. If everyone in the economy starts to simply extract from the earth and exploit the efforts of others through empty money, economy hollows out and collapses.

> *No amount of reform will help a system that rewards taking (squandering wealth) over giving (creating wealth). Such a system is fundamentally unsustainable. It will go bankrupt, despite all efforts to "extend and pretend." Transformation is required.*

Let's look at some examples of corrupted, "taking" economy:

- High-frequency traders have used high-powered computers to shift huge amounts of ones and zeroes in microseconds, guaranteeing a profit, and skewing the market.

- The huge private mortgage system, MERS, has seized the right to digitize ownership of real estate and allow itself to be used to transfer titles without filing legally required and authorized paperwork. As a result, clear ownership and title chains have been cast into doubt.

- Gross Domestic Product (GDP), the supposed lifeblood of the nation, is calculated by total spending (a form of taking). There is no distinction between healthy and unhealthy spending.

- Forms of giving, like donating and responsible saving either do not figure into GDP calculations or suppress level of GDP.

- Most current definitions of "standard of living" (higher material spending and use) are equated with "quality of life," ignoring environmental limits and research showing happiness does not correlate with material wealth.

- Solutions offered by both liberal and conservative economists emphasize increased consumer spending and jobs. Neither party acknowledges the irreversible disappearance of jobs due to outsourcing, automation, and productivity increase, nor admits the environmental lunacy of increasing consumption.

- Government programs for older generations like Medicare and Social Security have far outstripped the ability of younger generations to pay for them. Under current trends, older participants will receive more in benefits than they paid in. The difference is simply being made up in borrowing.

- Private banks are being rewarded with taxpayer bailouts for spectacular failure, for taking down the global financial system, and for being "too big to fail."

"Conventional wisdom" does not have the answers. This book will challenge these delusions and provide workable alternatives.

Applied effort in community + real value = transformed economy

I take no classic political side. Liberal welfare states and neo-conservative privatized state policies are both obsolete. They both operate by taking more than they give.

My orientation is one of *community*, where 1) people and organizations learn to prefer and derive greater fulfillment from giving, producing, and sharing and 2) greed is considered warped behavior. These communities, if linked and strong, can band together to coordinate resistance to corrupt larger-level practices and develop alternatives.

> *Why community? Community is where people can actually see and feel the worth of their applied effort, and thus feel drawn to give. Community is where real value is produced, exchanged, and felt. Community is also small enough to develop respectful intimacy, communication, and collaboration with neighbors.*

"Connected communities" are those that develop internal opportunities for individual achievement and shared success and external opportunities for collaboration with other communities over larger-level issues. The "individual" is too disconnected by him or herself without community, and "society" is too abstract without community.

So how does "community" help people learn to give, solve the "taking" problems identified above, and promote contributing and developing? (These will be elaborated further in this book). By...

- **Encouraging community cooperative exchanges,** like farmer's markets and tool libraries, which support more effective and efficient ways to share know-how and available social resources.

- **Developing circle lending and crowd funding,** which help cut out middlemen, by allowing people to pool their money to directly fund everything from home purchases to worthy creative projects.

- **Expanding the notion of "profit" beyond finance to include people and planet.** What are the best relationships between finance, community, and environment to maximize overall quality of life and prioritize human worth over net worth? This is reinforced by a notion of "optimum" life profit rather than "maximum" financial profit.

- **Recognizing non-material assets (creativity, community, entrepreneurialism, etc.) over material assets as the primary driver of quality of life.** Connected economy under this principle would seek to provide people with material opportunities and resources to maximize their non-material well-being.

- **Increasing sharing and decreasing consumption.** Car share, bike share, and cooperative living arrangements are just some of the ways people are realizing that they not only can save money, maintenance costs, time, and hassle, but can expand available opportunity to leave the "rat race" and pursue deeper talents.

- **Linking and meeting human needs directly, rather than waiting for some private or governmental agency.** Many emerging needs can be solved just by connecting them. For instance if you had unemployed youth assisting in elder care and being compensated in the food about to go past its due date, you could solve three problems in one stroke, need for care, need for work, and need to reduce waste. There are many other examples.

- **Emphasizing local and small business over huge unaccountable corporations.** If you have to look someone in the face day after day, you are much less likely to try to exploit them. Local labors of love require hard work, relationship-building, and ingenuity. Benefits directly reach people, provide work, and build good will.

Basically connected communities are about embracing the power of choice and exchange to co-create our lives.

THE FUTURE IS CONNECTED AND COLLABORATIVE

Armageddon talk will get us nowhere: "It's beyond repair. What is there to learn? It just needs to be torn down!" "We're screwed. The world is toast. Grab what you can, and protect yourself and your family. Buy guns, buy silver, buy gold, stock up on canned goods..."

Then what?

Like it or not, we are bound to each other in an unprecedented way. There are no long-lasting purely individual solutions. Lasting solutions from here on out are inextricably collaborative solutions. Should you prudently protect yourself from abuse? Yes, by all means. However, this is only part of the equation. Mere individual and family survival in the present will not ensure the future of your children's children.

Finding a vital, interactive, smart way to share is what will allow us to prosper long into the future. We are in a global world where our fates link. Neither toxic chemicals nor toxic financial practices respect boundaries. They have already found their way into practically every public space.

If the problem is public, the solution will have to be public. This is the hope of connected communities.

DEMOCRATIC CAPITALISM

This leaves us with one important question before we embark on our exploration: Can there be such a thing as democratic capitalism? Isn't capitalism inherently about taking and maximizing individual financial profit at the expense of others? "Aren't you really talking about some jazzed up form of communism or socialism?"

No, quite the opposite. Upon close examination democratic capitalism may be the only real capitalism out there and the most viable alternative to corrupted capitalism. Democratic capitalism in simple terms is "having money serve people." Corrupted capitalism is "having people serve money."

In other words, capitalist systems that personify money and objectify people are corrupted. (You see this in terms like "human capital.") Capitalist systems that respect people and objectify money (i.e. use currency as units of exchange to optimize well-being) have at least a chance of being connected and healthy.

Democratic capitalism is of, by, and for the people. Who else is the economy supposed to serve? The rich (plutocracy)? The state (socialism)? The ruling bureaucracy (communism)? The self-appointed elite (oligarchy)? Kings (monarchy)? Corporations (corporatocracy)? No. It is meant to serve you and me together.

> *We have never enacted democratic capitalism,*
> *and it is about high time we started*

From trillion dollar government welfare checks to crooked banks, to billion dollar subsidies of Big Oil (even when they were making record profits), to pork barrel goodies for a whole range of constituencies, the message up to now has been clear: "Get yours. Extract from everyone else."

No functioning system, much less capitalism, can run on that premise forever.

The fact that healthy democratic capitalism has never been enacted should not be a discouragement. We do not have the luxury of despair. We need to learn our historical lessons, take the best of current capitalism, and create what is essential for the future.

This is the purpose of *Transforming Economy: From Corrupted Capitalism to Connected Communities*.

I

CORRUPTED CAPITALISM

Learning From the Past

SUMMARY

> **Corrupted capitalism (def.):** "Having people serve money." Capitalist assumptions or systems that objectify people and personify money. Actions that give greater social rights to money than citizens. Examples: Corporate personhood, "Citizens United" Supreme Court case (which concluded money = speech), terms like "human capital," non-dischargeable student debt, too-big-too-fail bank bailouts.

Major points:

- Infinite growth is impossible in a finite system.

- There is no such real thing as "externalized" liability in a global system.

- Finance systems need to be straightforward and transparent. Now, they are not so.

- Debts themselves are not assets. Ability to pay debts is the asset.

- Money needs to circulate. Monopolies and concentrations of wealth ruin economies by binding up the flow of goods and services and freezing exchange.

- Without regulation and actual risk involving real consequences, the financial system and its leaders will continue to run wild.

- Gambling involves money changing hands. Money taken out of a system through misrepresentation of value is not gambling; it is theft and fraud.

- The alleged complexity of the financial system serves a very simple purpose: To ensure the most favorable conditions for risk-free and fraudulent profit.

- Any asset whose value is "unknowable" is either worthless, fake, or both.

- Assets cannot be "toxic." Anything toxic is a liability. Toxic liabilities are those that cannibalize value by poisoning both the holder and the surrounding system.

- Integrity is the linchpin of sound economics.

- Functioning capitalism requires that those who take risks both gain and lose on their merits. Without this, there is no need for merit or propriety.

- Capital must have reference in real assets for it to have worth.

Fundamental challenges:

- Economic bets have exceeded the value of the assets they refer to.

- People still tend to make their meaning and choices based upon limited, compartmentalized knowledge. Even educated, tech-literate people rarely see how their perceptions, assumptions, and methods connect in the big picture.

- "Shadow banking" is unregulated, non-transparent, and unaccountable private banking but still receives public benefits and guarantees, creating an incentive for counterfeit value and fraud.

- Financial derivatives appear to have no clear definition or discernible value origin. Are they are capital vehicles, insurance vehicles, investment vehicles, all three, or none of the above? What are they backed by?

- There have been no prosecutions or serious investigations of even obvious systemic high-level financial fraud. World governments appear to have decided to protect, rather than prosecute, financial criminals.

- Environmentally, financially, and spiritually we cannot continue to simply materially grow and consume.

- We no longer have a global financial system tethered to concrete reality. Value has migrated from something you can earn and use, to abstract "references to value," based on concocted claims.

- The current global financial system makes it possible for powerful players to 1) make up their own rules to maximize self-interest, 2) establish the value of their own assets, 3) inflate that value based on estimated future returns, 4) leverage inflated value to make huge gambles, 5) lean on taxpayer bailouts when in trouble, and 6) do this without any disclosure or accountability.

- What we have now is worse than "moral hazard." Not only do players escape punishment for doing the wrong thing, but they have active, rational incentives to do the wrong thing in order to maximize profit.

- "Maximizing (financial) profit" has been allowed to gain an unreferenced power without balance, challenge, or duty, to social and environmental well-being.

- Maximization of growth at any cost creates a cancer-like condition because no distinction is made between healthy and unhealthy growth.

- We cannot live on economic bets. We require healthy air, food, water, reasonable housing, and effective health care to live.

Proactive alternatives:

- Require corporations, chartered by the public, to conduct themselves in accordance with public regulation and well-being or lose their charter.

- Eliminate corporate personhood. Corporations should not be considered persons nor enjoy the attendant rights of citizens.

- Prevent practices which privatize benefit and publicize risk. Levy transaction taxes on free-wheeling trading. Link financial officers' private credit liability to their professional financial decisions. Small business owners are often forced to.

- Rewrite bankruptcy laws so that citizens, including students, who legitimately fail on the private level can get back on their feet publicly. Two-thirds of personal bankruptcies result from divorce, job loss, or failure of health.

- Reinforce public policy that rewards long-term quality over short-term quantity. Currently the "maximum profit" meme that drives big business injects incentives to cut corners and think short term.

- Sponsor grass-roots discussion and development of a "good life" that emphasizes involvement, participation, and investment of time, talent, treasure and trust above "getting mine," speculative investing, and early retirement.

- Use microfinance, community, and small business models as templates for bigger operations.

- Invest real money and commitment into developing non-scarce, non-polluting assets, like community, creativity, and learning, that have intrinsic (rather than simply instrumental) worth and that increase in value the more they are shared.

- Ask and pursue the foundational questions: "What is the economy and society meant to serve? What is most fulfilling and important in life?"

- Aristotle said, "We are what we repeatedly do." Do we like what we repeatedly do and who we are as a result? If not, we need ways to change what we do and who we are in the world to reflect our deeper sensibilities and commitments.

1

IMAGINARY WORTH, EMPIRE OF DEBT

*How Modern Finance Created
its Own Downfall*

I wrote the original pieces of this article in 2008. In 2013 this essay has actually become more relevant. The fundamental flaws I identify remain unresolved and, indeed, have worsened. Official global financial policies have ignored these identified flaws, preventing accountability and encouraging further abuse. I bring them forth now to help you take genuine stock of our current reality, understand what has led up to it, and look toward viable options.

How did we get here? The current global financial unraveling and meltdown have brought us face-to-face with a stark and uncomfortable truth: with all its reassuring numbers, our financial system is a human system, based on human frailties and desires, resting almost completely upon imaginary notions of worth.

Historical financial innovations have led us piece by piece into a phase shift from ownership of real assets to concocted wealth that no longer has a credible connection to productivity, life needs, or the day-to-day requirements of commerce.

Historically, we have moved from the bartering of material goods and services, to the convenient exchange of dollars no longer backed by anything but faith, to "creative" financial vehicles (i.e. derivatives) that leverage symbolic wealth to create infinite paper profits not actually connected to anything real.

In so doing, we have progressively departed from the foundation of what was once considered financial worth—the competent stakeholdership, ownership, and stewardship of real property involving labor, earnings, investment, risk, reward, and responsibility.

We've reached the "asymptote," the mathematical limit whereby even an infinite increase in concocted value produces no growth of worth on the real level.

We are now caught in a circle of absurdity— lending and borrowing derived from credit derived from collateral derived from inflated assets derived from future returns derived from "marked to model" theoretical value derived from unlimited growth and ability to pay.

This last assumption is not only wrong but could never be right. The pyramid scheme has reached its limit.

> *Finite goods cannot play out in infinite terms.*

This problem has come from humans imposing upon the world an economic mindset built around maximizing profit through extraction, exploitation, and concentration of wealth. Profits have become increasingly dependent on maximum short-term competitive returns driving greater and more efficient exploitation.

Much like a biological cancer single-mindedly programmed to take over the body, rogue financial instruments and players that mindlessly aim for growth at all costs have saturated the global system.

Faced with the limits of growth to real wealth, the financial system has manufactured a parallel "shadow banking system" that creates "value" out of thin air by simply fabricating, assigning, and exchanging it. This has culminated in markets for so-called "derivatives" (to be explained later) that have exceeded a quadrillion (a thousand trillion) dollars.

Many of those trillions in derivatives involve credit default "swaps" (CDSs), an unregulated insurance, which is the subject of the following essays.

FINANCIAL TRICKERY VS. NATURAL AND MATHEMATICAL LAWS

In the following essays I also point to several basic natural laws of systems, that have been simply ignored or overridden in the greed-driven frenzy to manufacture growth:

Infinite growth is impossible in a finite system.

Real worth cannot simply be fabricated from nothing and anointed as having value. One can be very creative about assigning worth and developing unlimited growth in assigned worth, but real worth remains constrained to its mooring: Can it create quality of life? Can it feed, shelter, and clothe? Can it produce clean air and water? Can it create lasting fulfillment?

Even the magic of percentages and myths about "houses always going up in value" assume unlimited growth in environmental and financial systems with limits. Infinite growth premises are demonstrably false in finite systems.

What they really communicate is this: "Let the next generation deal with the consequences as long as I get my maximum returns now." Infinite growth *can* happen in non-finite, non-material systems, and I indicate some of those possibly pro-social non-finite systems of exchange toward the end of this chapter.

There is no such real thing as "externalized" liability in a global system.

As with the exploitation of natural resources, there is always a cost to any action that seeks to extract value. Someone has to pay the price. The more interconnected a system, the more readily and strongly that price will turn up to affect all the players including the initial beneficiaries.

Finance systems need to be straightforward and transparent.

This one would seem a no-brainer, but objectively speaking, non-transparency, rather than transparency, has been central to late capitalism, aiding concentration of wealth and enabling the unfair and sometimes illegal benefit of some players at the expense of others. Furthermore, this is not just about something obvious like insider trading.

Corporations have started shell companies to hide off-the-balance deficits. As explained in these essays, financial institutions have marked their assets "to (their own) model" without fully revealing their assumptions.

Corporate bond rating agencies have assessed junk bonds as AAA, facilitating the sale of junk bonds to pension funds, who were only interested in secure investments. All this has been hidden behind so-called "complexity" (a mantra repeated brainlessly in the media), a Rube Goldberg device of financial levers whose sole real purpose was to hide unscrupulous and unreasonable practices.

Debts are not assets.

As I explain in many of my articles, buying debt can appear to be a good investment on paper, but this rests on ability to pay. When debts are so constructed to create unreasonable re-payment (fast accelerating interest and principal payments rapidly outstripping the equity of collateral) they will fail.

Monopolies and concentrations of wealth ruin economies by binding up the flow of goods and services and freezing exchange.

Healthy systems both natural and financial depend upon high diversity and exchange among distinct entities each offering something of real value. This is why a rain forest is considered a very rich system—many niches, many species all participate in the web of life.

This is why Henry Ford said he needed to make his wages high enough and his cars cheap enough for his own workers to buy them. This is why a large middle class is the bedrock of a functioning democracy.

As I mention in the following essays, debt instruments have the effect of swallowing the normal citizen and worker's paycheck, paralyzing his or her ability to *spend* after the *borrowing* value of his or her assets (i.e. houses) is tapped out.

This has been exacerbated in America by declining real wages, non-compensated increased productivity, and outsourced jobs. This has been further demonstrated by banks' unwillingness to lend to each other. When the flow of money stops, financial systems seize up.

Without regulation and actual risk involving real consequences, the financial system and its leaders will run wild.

This one would again seem to be obvious, yet this law has been ignored as well. Myths about the ability of a market, based on greed and acquisition, to regulate itself do not make any sense. Yet the world system, and in particular the American system driven by neo-conservative ideology, hailed deregulation as the triumph of "freedom."

Chief executive officers of large corporations could take huge risks for their companies and reap hundreds of millions of dollars in salaries and bonuses if those risks paid, or completely ruin their companies through failed risk and get golden parachutes worth "only" tens of millions of dollars.

Reckless behavior is guaranteed if it is rewarded more than prudent, intelligent behavior in an economic system. From an acquisition standpoint, this is individually "rational" behavior, even though it is unhealthy and irrational from a system standpoint.

Why is this irrationality allowed to go on unchecked?

The question might be asked, "Why were all these very simple and obvious maxims ignored? What were people thinking?" I think much of it centers around the fact that people's education and identity still has its roots in a long-past industrial age.

> *People still tend to make their meaning and choices based upon largely near-sighted, compartmentalized, and stratified knowledge.*

Even well educated people rarely look deeply into the big picture and to whether their particular perceptions, assumptions, and knowledge reasonably fit with other parts of a system. Generally, if we can make some money, feed our families, and have some fun, we don't really care what the system is doing.

Now, this big picture "system" understanding is becoming a necessity in our day-to-day decisions, and it is emerging as critical to a long-term functioning global economy. Financial role-players have lost this big picture by competitively narrowing their specialties until they have lost all context in the push to extract another penny.

I build my analysis from the big picture in conversation with important specific evidence. My background includes a Ph.D. in philosophy of education, an emphasis in cultural studies and psychology, and a natural sciences and math undergraduate background. This has allowed me to gain the tools to look at systems and the specialized skills to examine the various parts of systems.

Natural sciences have helped me to apprehend existing systems, both natural and human. Psychology has helped me to investigate motive. Philosophy has led me to question assumptions and test "common sense" thinking. Cultural studies have prepared me to understand context. Mathematics knowledge has allowed me to check the actual numbers and formulas that financial systems are using.

It is my hope that these essays and my analysis can help revive an integrated, imaginative, and critical examination and creation of the world around us.

Part I: Credit Default Swaps: A 70 Trillion Dollar Counterfeiting Ring

The market [leading up to the 2008 crash] for so-called "credit default swaps" was nearly equal to the total global GDP (http://www.isda.org/statistics/pdf/ISDA-Market-Survey-annual-data.pdf). This amount was about 60-70 trillion dollars in notional value by most estimates.

Yet these "complex" derivatives have no discernible "origin" or value. People aren't sure whether they are capital vehicles, insurance vehicles, investment vehicles, all three, or none of the above. What is becoming very clear, however, is that they, along with many of the other "creative" financial vehicles are nothing more than a bold mass-counterfeiting scheme based on a very simple premise and set of conditions.

Their values are not "unknowable," as some have claimed. We know what their values are—worthless. Our problem is that we're not willing to acknowledge this and accept the social or personal ramifications. The bald truth is harder for most to bear than the big lie.

What if you tried to buy food at a grocery store with cash you withdrew from a bank, and found out that the money was counterfeit? (This receiving fake money from a real bank has actually happened: http://www.huffingtonpost.com/2012/06/04/td-bank-counterfeit-bills_n_1567745.html).

You worked for that money, provided labor, goods, etc., and you got worthless paper in return. You offered something that had real value in return for something you thought had value but did not. Either you swallow the rip-off and lose real value or someone covers for you—the government, insurance, etc.

What happens if this worthless scrip you receive takes the form of digital funny money, concocted out of thin air, without any real assets or capital to back it up? What happens if the global market for this worthless scrip exceeds the world's GDP? Oops, there is no one who could possibly cover that. No bailout can buy up tens of trillions of dollars of counterfeit currency or phantom assets.

If I promise to ensure you against loss, and I have no actual resources to back it up other than a contract that says I will, I have produced a counterfeit document. My promise has to be backed by an ability to pay, and I don't have it. What I have are phony assets, "marked to model," acquired by selling off the risk of my guarantee to someone else, who in turn does the same.

I take your money and leverage it into risky investments including more exotic vehicles that have no value, but that I think/pretend have value.

> *This is not gambling. This is simple theft.*
> *In gambling, money comes and goes, but is essentially conserved somewhere. With theft, money is taken out of the system and hidden.*

In this system of massive counterfeiting and theft, I do the equivalent of flooding the monetary system with fraudulent promissory notes, passed off as assets, while skimming huge transaction fees.

Yes, debt has now magically become an asset because it can ostensibly generate interest payment income and fees. So we lower the monthly minimum on credit cards and jack up the interest rate to keep up the charade of huge returns. We allow negative amortization. We promote "balloon payments."

There is no real value there *by design*. There cannot be. No one can possibly pay off a mortgage that is ten times his or her income with a principal that actually increases over time. But if you can pass off the personal or institutional liability, you may be able to "escape" accountability and profit from this scam.

As a *system*, however, this will inevitably fail, and, as we are seeing with both ecological and financial environments, we are all part of a system where even "externalized" liabilities will return to bite us. (Note: "Risk" assumes some possibility of positive actual return. "Liability" is simply a minus.)

What happens when a country floods its own monetary system with currency or makes money far too cheap through lowered interest rates. At first rampant inflation occurs in things like stocks or house prices, as demand for goods is driven up. Anyone can buy anything with his or her own credit leverage and a lack of fear of consequences.

Then devaluation and deflation emerge as fundamentals catch up, followed by a liquidity crisis due to exposed (fraudulent) leverages— leverages, which are composed of essentially infinite multiplication of pseudo value in exotic financial vehicles.

What happens when you flood the global market with toxic debt that far exceeds the ability of any country, and even consortiums of companies or countries, to address the issue? You have a global meltdown, or you try to stave off the inevitable reckoning with 700 billion dollar band-aids that have within their conduct of use no provisions for transparency, because that transparency would expose the far deeper and more widespread fraud under the symptoms.

In the end, no matter the route, what you find is worthless garbage.

We've been here before. We've been told that terrorists flying planes into buildings were "unthinkable," requiring complex planning and massive funding. It was not unthinkable or complex. It was simple, needing only a coordinated plan to destroy buildings, exploited vulnerabilities, flight training, box cutters, and navigation skills.

We were warned of a "mushroom cloud," in Iraq along with bio-weapons and other complex threats that would threaten us if unlimited military powers were not extended the U.S. president.

It wasn't true or complex. In fact, we have solid testimony from sources to Pulitzer Prize-winning reporter Ron Suskind, that the government actually forged documents to make that case for war (http://www.nbcnews.com/id/26044443/). People lied to gain power, plain and simple, making us all pay again.

Now we have counterfeiting to the tune of trillions of dollars, and we're being asked [in 2008] to give 700 billion dollars to be used without any transparency, oversight, or accountability by Treasury Secretary Henry Paulson and Federal Reserve Chairman Ben Bernanke.

Well we know one way it will likely be used based on past conduct—to shroud the underlying core financial and moral crises...

[Update 2013: Has anything changed? No. My prediction proved correct and remains unfortunately so to this day in the form of "extend and pretend" money printing and debt restructuring and a complete absence of investigations or notable criminal prosecutions in the financial industry.]

It's time we stop dragging it out. It's time we make a clean honest break so we can deal with the reality, feel the pain, assess the damage, and make a new start as more informed people.

This is what this book will help do.

Part II: How the Credit Default Swap Scam Works

Remember in math, when they gave you a very complex looking figure and told you to find the geometric area. The worker bees in class would try to figure out all the many angles and tally up the area *inside* the figure. This almost always led to careless errors or took too long to solve the problem given a limited test-taking time.

The implicit lesson was to find the answer by drawing a regular figure (most often a rectangle) *around* the complex figure, calculating its easy-to-compute area, and *subtracting* the areas that constituted the difference between the two figures. Voila... easy, fast, elegant and accurate.

I think the same lesson can be applied to credit default swaps [and other derivatives]. Instead of asking the obvious, complex, and obscuring question, "What value *do* they have?", one should ask the elegant and simple question, "What value *could* they have?" Even a cursory examination would seem to indicate that the answer is either zero or less-than-zero.

This comes from the interaction between debts and fees. In practice the greater the debt serviced (again concocted as if it had value), the greater the fee that would accrue in real terms to servicers.

Again this debt is curiously cast as an asset, often in ways that were supported by nothing other than increasing future returns that assume unlimited resources and continuing ability to pay. One would have hoped that the dot com bubble would have laid to rest the notion of hyped future returns as a good basis to assign value.

Now we go to the 60 - 70 trillion dollar credit default swap market of 2007. If only one to two percent "service fee" were charged in these transactions (which are based on illusory assets), we're talking nearly three-quarters to one-and-a-half *trillion* dollars in real term fees being siphoned off the global economy for no productive purpose.

If these fees are attached to phony assets, as I have propounded, than that means a net loss, a trillion dollars of capital, taken right out of the system. No wonder we have a liquidity crisis!

Here is how the scam seems to work. Insure credit default with inadequate capital, assuming the market will always go up. I've heard actual figures quoted in various finance magazine articles that fly-by-night operations were insuring billions of dollars of debt in major banks with only millions of dollars of collateral.

So we're talking a tenth of a percent reserve, not ten percent, and the more exotic instruments apparently had no reserve or used the reserve to leverage other risky investments. As the market goes up, everybody's happy. Everybody appears to be making a killing, much like a pyramid scheme... *as long as you can get the next person to pay.* So now someone defaults in real terms, make that several million people. There aren't anything but IOUs in the system *that have been treated as assets and capital.*

There is no money.

This is why I say that toxic assets may be toxic, but they are not assets, and that they have zero value and actually less-than-zero value. If I have insured against loss with only a tenth-of-a-percent reserve, and yet I am charging a percent or two per year for my services, I'm actually charging ten times more than I can actually pay out in case of a default. Those fees were not going into the reserve but into the pockets of the servicers.

The posturing by Treasury Secretary Henry Paulson in 2008 appeared to be an attempt to shroud the scamming through January, 2009, allowing him (and the Bush, Jr. administration) to duck out, and temporarily save his friends and colleagues in the banking business. It follows a CEO pattern that has been going on since Reagan's deregulatory days.

We saw it in Enron. "Don't get left holding the bag. Let it blow up on someone else's watch."

We likely have been ripped off trillions of dollars. Seven hundred billion dollars of even real money won't fix the problem (never mind that the this 700 billion is simply more debt added to the global system on America's behalf).

As "Devilstower" commented in an excellent diary post on Kos,

> Is it altogether a good idea to run up debts exceeding all assets it is even *possible* to own?" (http://devilstower.dailykos.com/storyonly/2008/9/21/9322/74248/245/602838)

[Update 2013: This initial plan to extend the entire financial charade beyond the 2008 U.S. presidential election did not work and exerted a huge influence on the results. Bear Stearns and Lehman Brothers fell. AIG hit an iceberg, and the entire global financial system was thrown into a turmoil that still exists today in masked form.]

Part III: Credit Default Swaps Create Less-Than-Zero Value

First, let us establish that "credit default swaps" (CDS's) are an unregulated form of credit default insurance that had to be titled "swap" (a trading term) to avoid being regulated like actual insurance. Because it was unregulated, there were no capital reserve requirements, that is, no money was required to be held to pay out if someone actually does default.

So CDS's could easily be counterfeit documents guarding against risk without any collateral. So at best they are worthless, and with a 60 - 70 trillion dollar market in counterfeit goods, it is safe to say we are in trouble without some way to re-scale assets distorted by the introduction of counterfeit financial instruments.

Now, how can a supposed "asset" like credit default swaps have a "less-than-zero" (negative) value. First, credit default swaps were and are insuring debt. Debt is not an asset as I explained in previous essays, but a liability. Mistake number one was to confuse asset and liability. These debts *are treated as assets* because *in theory* they produced interest income and transaction or service fee income at pretty high initial rates of return (based on the inflated value growth of housing, for instance).

Unfortunately, many financial models have no contact with reality. They assume unlimited growth and ability to pay. When matched against the reality of people paying ten times their salary for houses that actually added more money owed to their mortgage principal (i.e. with negative amortization), required no money down, and set up "balloon payments," large step-ups in payments after a few years) there is no possible way borrowers could not default in a predictable span of time.

Even someone without math training could see that the fundamentals were way off leading up to the housing crash and that the assumptions had to be false, *but* those profiting did not care. "Mark to model" (or "mark to fantasy" as some have called it) trumped "mark to market" or "mark to reality", allowing maximum short-term paper returns in a system run by greed that created phony prosperity down the line.

Rating agencies gained big money. Moody's and Standard & Poor's garnered huge fees for rating junk as AAA, the highest rating. Big investment banks and hedge funds were able to "socialize the liability and privatize the gain". Loose-lending mortgage brokers piled up the commissions.

Housing prices were way off the historical mean, with mortgage payments three times what it would cost to rent the same house in California, for instance. Again it does not take a math genius or a clairvoyant to see that these out-of-whack trends would lead to a crash. When fundamentally unsupported buying frenzies reach certain critical levels in volume and price, no amount of default insurance will be enough.

- If you spend good money for an insurance policy against debt default (or fire damage, or anything) and the policy pays you nothing when catastrophe does in fact happen, *the value of that policy is zero.*

- If you pay premiums, maintenance, or transaction fees to keep that worthless policy active, you have *less-than-zero value:* the money you spent into the policy could have been invested elsewhere or even held under a mattress and still retained some value.

- If you own a chunk of a credit default swap market as part of your portfolio, it is even worse: you have something that is worthless (has zero value), upon which you are paying premiums (less-than-zero value), and which is actively sabotaging by its very pernicious presence in the market the real value of other parts of your portfolio *(worse than less-than-zero value).* As anyone who has an index fund can attest, the Dow Jones lost a third of its value in just a half-year or so in large part because of the overall uncertainty about value created by CDS's.

Put it this way, store money in a government insured CD and you get to keep the value of your principal and a return (positive value + return).

Keep the money under a mattress and you retain the principal, somewhat devalued by inflation, but still largely retaining its positive value. If you keep the money under your mattress and your bed burns down, you are left with zero value. If you pay someone to insure your money, your bed burns down, and they don't pay out, you have less-than-zero value.

> *With CDS's, it is the equivalent of paying an arsonist to set fire to your house, burning it, your bed, and your money, to the ground. This is what I mean by "worse than less-than-zero value."*

I intuit that part of the liquidity problem right now is that counterfeit assets (CDS's, etc.) were traded for hard assets (cash, etc.) and promptly stashed in non-transparent accounts to "lock in" gains and hide the assets.

Part of the clean-up of this global, criminal enterprise will have to involve auditing Swiss and other "off shore" bank accounts (where I would not be surprised to see trillions of dollars of cash have been stashed), private equity funds, hedge funds, and the like.

[Update 2013: This prediction I made in 2008 was confirmed in recent studies showing up to 32 trillion dollars are being held in offshore accounts: http://www.huffingtonpost.com/2012/07/22/super-rich-off-shore-havens_n_1692608.html and http://www.globalresearch.ca/the-global-elite-are-hiding-18-trillion-dollars-in-offshore-banks/5317691)]

Part IV: There Is Ultimately No Gaming the System: When the Micro Crash Reflects the Macro Crash

The 2008 seven hundred billion dollar U.S. banking bailout cannot really "work" from a system level. You have the same problem in macro that homeowners have in micro. Nobody knows what homes are worth right now, so buyers are sitting it out. It isn't about restricted credit (even though that is a factor).

[Update 2013: Houses are still being kept off the market and they have still not been valued at "marked to market". The game of "extend and pretend continues on its fifth year.]

It isn't about being too cash strapped to make a down payment (though that too is a factor). It's about not wanting to be suckered into buying something that may still be overpriced. All the fundamentals indicate that houses have quite a bit further to dip to reach the historical mean (the inflation index), so that hesitation is perfectly well-founded.

Treasury Secretary Henry Paulson wanted to put up 700 billion dollars in money to keep propping up assets that have no discernible value, and gallingly, openly lobbied to have his banking friends receive fees for managing the government's purchase and management of toxic assets using this money.

Money needs to circulate.

You cannot have a financial *system* that works like this, where certain people, especially though suspect means, extract all the capital in a system for their own profit and leave nothing to others. That's why having a huge middle class in democratic economies is so successful and wealth inequality is so damaging.

However, we also have large numbers of homeowners now who have tapped ("ATMed") the illusory equity created by massively increased home "values" (created by cheap money and a fraudulence-driven demand for home-buying), in a mirror action of the "big boy" traders and managers who siphoned off huge amounts of money in transaction and management fees.

You would almost have to have homeowners and hedge fund managers put back in the money that they took out. Homeowners have spent it to buoy a phony economy (like good "patriotic" citizens), and hedge fund managers and other members of the financial elite have either hidden it or lost part of it into worthless vehicles, which they are apparently trying to recover by using the taxpayer as the fall guy.

Homeowners largely cannot give this money back and wealthy people apparently will not. The liquidity problem, I suspect, comes from the world's financial elite being unwilling to take their money out of hiding and to disclose (for financial and criminal prosecution reasons) what "instruments" they have concocted to suck in other people's money. No one wants to take the fall and face accountability.

However, U.S. taxpayers, for instance, have negative savings. So 700 billion dollar injection of "cash" is itself an illusion. This "value" is just more debt added to a ledger supposedly backed by U.S.'s historically secure economic system. But for the last 30 years the American economy itself has been increasingly tethered to financial services based on the illusion of debt-as-asset.

We would have to raise taxes and extract that money from people's actual paychecks for it to be real and that would cause a huge downturn in consumer spending and ruin the economy another way, given its present model.

This is why taxing the heck out of people who made a suspect or corrupt profit out of this mess makes sense, both the assets and the income and the transactions themselves. If you want to make illusory instruments and extract value, then we'll tax you a quarter percent to make the transaction and 30% of your take and an additional percentage to hold and maintain assets in the public trust.

That would stop a lot of the thievery right there. Make a real-term consequence to a phony asset, and you'll find a lot of people stop this creative accounting, because they don't have even a fraction of the cash necessary to do their crooked business.

There is no doubt in my mind that large corporations, many of whom pay no taxes, used these same illusory instruments to concoct losses (which they are allowed to deduct) to escape paying their fair share of taxes to society.

But presently we are at a standstill with no real way out, except together, if we recognize and treat this all truly as a system.

I anticipate massive debt forgiveness will become a reality.

You can't move when your debt swallows your entire paycheck, and this condition now presides on a global scale. Since much global debt is based on fraud, debt forgiveness and better auditing would be acts of necessity, rather than merely altruism and good governance. This also opens the door to economies switching to a more qualitative and non-material basis of worth and well-being. [These concepts are discussed and developed in detail, later in this book.]

Environmentally, financially, and spiritually we can't continue to simply materially grow and consume. We need to invest real money and commitment into developing non-scarce, non-polluting assets that have intrinsic (rather than simply instrumental) worth and actually increase in value the more they are shared.

I foresee community and learning as possible goods that fit these criteria. Intercultural exchange of music, language, and appreciation might be others.

Lastly, I think we will need huge investments in infrastructure and ingenuity, including communication networks, social media, alternative energy, and so forth. These will both enhance the ability to develop non-scarce, non-material goods, but also support a new basis for the physical economy.

This movement is possible now, and many people are already making the move. It will be interesting to see if the present extended crisis contributes or detracts from the shift.

Part V: Toxic Liabilities are Not Assets

I received a very good question from a reader of the above essays. He said he understood why credit default swaps were valueless, given no collateral backup, but he had two main areas of questioning:

1) Can't there still be liability for *the writer* of a credit default swap if the purchaser makes a valid claim? Won't they have to pay or go bankrupt?

2) How can debt not be an asset?

In the reader's words:

> If I were to owe you a million dollars and offered you a choice between a piece of real estate conservatively valued at that figure and a valid promissory note for like amount signed by Warren Buffet, wouldn't you at least think about taking the "debt" as opposed to the asset? What am I missing here?"

Here was my response:

First, credit default swaps (CDS's) have produced exactly that bankruptcy scenario to which the reader pointed. Many of the fly-by-night operators that originated and/or peddled CDS's did go bankrupt. They simply made promises to cover defaults without adequate capitalization or collateral. Their companies were essentially shells, which leveraged paper phantom assets as if they were real assets.

These smaller companies could not pay so they went out of business, as did many fly-by-night mortgage companies. This did not stop them from siphoning off huge personal incomes and fees before their companies went bankrupt. [That is just stealing money. Again, there have been no criminal prosecutions of the big companies on this.]

Since the personal liability (bankruptcy, etc.) of the owners of those companies is not tied to the performance of the company, they simply were able to take the money and run.

> *This becomes a theme—big short-term returns, no personal consequence, and "externalized liability" by people who don't really have a stake in the matter.*

Two, the bigger companies (as in Lehman Brothers, AIG, Citigroup, Goldman Sachs, etc.) did not do their due diligence on CDS's and should have eaten their losses associated with CDS's. If they did not understand these financial instruments, they should not have bought them [or created them].

However, they did buy [and create] many CDS's in their greed-driven frenzy to cover their own skyrocketing short-term returns in risky markets (i.e. sub-prime). To fully reveal and write down those losses would be to show how undercapitalized they are, send their stock prices plummeting, and guarantee their bankruptcies as well, with results that would ripple through the entire market.

This would affect and has affected necessary short-term lending and borrowing in the broader economy like those loans extended to regular, productive businesses to ensure they meet payroll. Big banks and investment houses were deemed "too big to fail" and were not allowed to go bankrupt (except for Lehman Brothers), because the ripple effect was considered too dire. [In 2013 this, again, has not changed. The too-big-to-fail banks are even bigger.]

However, this commitment sets up another serious systemic jeopardy that is far greater than "moral hazard." Now non-transparency is used to shore up markets and avoid panics, allowing private banks to self-assign any value they choose to their junk assets and then sell those assets to governmental central banks at the chosen price!

Hence we see a short-sighted and corrupt plan by Henry Paulson to have the U.S. government simply absorb private "toxic assets," take them off the books with taxpayer money, and "make it all go away."

This will not work since there are tens of trillions of dollars of toxic liabilities (do not call them assets) in the form of CDS's and other derivatives, not simply a couple hundred billion. Sub-prime loans are not the source of this problem. It is the leveraging of sub-prime loans that is the problem.

Too-clever-by-half, handsome, Ivy League-schooled power brokers are the ones creating the problems. Poor people, including minorities, who got in over their heads in trying to own homes are not to blame, notwithstanding lawmakers' attempts to assign them blame. We could simply buy up defaulted mortgages for that 700 billion dollars, and get at least 30-40% of our money back.

Answer this, how could any true asset be "toxic"

Houses, sub-prime or otherwise, have at least some worth, even if they have lost a good deal of their value. Precipitous losses happen in stock markets all the time.

However, as I explained in my essays, the leveraging of these mortgages *is* toxic and *is not* an asset, since it is simply a fabrication of value with no real backing. This leveraging truly poisons the economic system by diluting the worth of real assets and by calling into question the veracity of any claim of value.

Sooner or later we have to recognize a massive fraud has been perpetrated. It needs to be revealed that major companies have trillions of dollars of junk on their books and are likely not solvent according to traditional notions of solvency.

So we have a Catch-22, but not one that will be solved by hiding: Expose the fraud and risk likely short-term collapse and re-scaling of economic confidence and systems, or cover the symptoms, hide the toxins, and allow them to fester and rot out the economy in a prolonged sickness that may spread and gain momentum beyond attempts to assuage the problems. [2013, and the clock is still ticking.]

Regarding the reader's question about whether debt can be an asset:

> *"Your" ability to pay "me" (or confer to me something of equal or greater value to cover your debt) is the asset not your actual debt to me.*

If you borrowed a million dollars from me and gave me a choice of receiving real estate "conservatively valued" at a million dollars or a "valid" promissory note signed by Warren Buffet, you bet I would consider both and extend the loan to you on either account.

Both have substantial backing, not simply promises, but actual assets that have sound, plausible present and future value. Now if you gave me the choice of real estate, whose value was inflated to three times what a rental market could support by an appraiser you hired, and/or if you gave me a promissory note signed by Jeffrey Skilling of Enron fame, I'd tell you to take a walk.

The key phrases uttered by the reader were "conservatively valued" and "valid". Both indicate that the collateral provided to me for my loan are "real" and not simply contrived. Neither value is inflated, and both conform to tried-and-true market fundamentals.

If the money I lent to you was counterfeit, or the "asset" you offered as collateral was contrived, that would corrupt the system of borrowing and lending. It would destroy trust and reward deception. In a word, it would show, both in the positive and negative case, that sound markets run on integrity. The reader assumes this integrity in his/ her question. Evidence suggests that the present system does not have this integrity.

INTEGRITY IS THE LINCHPIN OF SOUND ECONOMICS

Integrity [even more than trust] is the basis of all sound valuation of currency and assets. Warren Buffett has made a career, many billions of dollars, and impressive returns for his investors by researching and rewarding integrity—companies who are productive, follow good business practices, offer something of real value, and address real needs for customers.

His reputation has been built on his integrity, his performance, and his candid analysis of the potential of companies. Moody's and Standard and Poor's, in contrast, have wasted whatever reputation they had by rating junk as AAA, something that could have been revealed simply by investigating what real assets these ratings were based upon.

> Rule: *If you can't explain to me the assets,*
> *then they are crap.*

[Update 2013: Warren Buffet's reputation, at least with me, took a beating when he invested in corrupt big banks, relying on U.S. government guarantees to make a tidy profit. That is not anywhere close to democratic capitalism.]

Other essential economic "system" assets deriving from integrity include sound regulation; enforcement of laws and contracts; punishment of violators; tax incentives for pro-social, responsible financial behavior; an effective judicial, legislative, and executive government which guarantees the rule of law; a functioning democracy; a large and healthy middle class; and an attitude and practice of care for each other.

All of these system assets have taken a beating in the U.S. from Ronald Reagan's presidential term onward (including Bill Clinton, frankly). Cowboy investing has been rewarded. The rule of law has been deemed "quaint" even in areas like the torture of prisoners. Regulatory agencies are staffed by industry lobbyists committed to de-regulation. Certain fundamentalist Christianity asserts that God favors the wealthy rather than the poor.

In each of these a "prosperity gospel" has emerged that subverts sound notions of value: "By virtue of having lots of money by whatever means, you are by nature upright, good, and just," rather than "By your virtue, intelligence, ingenuity, and integrity, you develop sound practices, products, and plans, that generate well-earned money."

In this sense, though I am a committed progressive socially and politically, I honor and agree with a traditional foundation and understanding of economic value. Perhaps it was my days growing up on a farm requiring productivity, hard work, and knowing b.s. when I stepped in it.

If a whole economic system loses its integrity, the phrase "buyer beware" loses its meaning. If my pension managers bought junk they were assured was secure investment by supposedly reputable experts, who do I trust now?

CREATING NEW PUBLIC POLICIES TO STRENGTHEN ECONOMIC INTEGRITY

We need to construct an economic system, which puts integrity into the driver's seat. This will mean more than criminal prosecutions, as necessary as those may be. This will mean identifying and rooting out the rot in the system that rewards irresponsibility.

This will mean admitting the ways in which we have all aided and abetted this theft and corruption of value. This will mean we acknowledge and support examples of economic exchange that have retained integrity and good sense.

Proposition One: I think it is high time we rigorously re-visit the notion of public charters for corporations. If corporations are chartered by the public, then they need to be both answerable to and regulated by that public. There should be no unregulated, quasi-regulated, or self-regulated publicly chartered companies.

I don't have a problem with unchartered privately administered companies. If a hedge fund or private equity firm wants to take private funds (and that means only personal private funds, no public pension fund money, for instance), then they should be allowed to do so with no guarantee from the public or for their investors.

If they gain, they gain; if they lose, they lose. If fraud happens, then investors can sue and/or press criminal charges. Any public business done by an unchartered company would be audited to ensure real assets back that business and guarantee primary public standing for repayment in any downturn.

Proposition Two: We should revisit the public/private dynamic regarding distribution of risk. Current laws and practices seem to favor a system that privatizes benefits and publicizes liability. Presently any person can set up an unregulated, dummy company (i.e. a mortgage or brokerage firm), use it to essentially fence financial goods (i.e. bad loans or CDS's) and then sell them off.

This "any person" can also skim off huge fees and salaries, and just walk away when the company goes bankrupt without any consequence—no injury to personal credit score, no requirement to give back ill-gotten wealth, etc.

If there was a tax on these free-wheeling deals, and if financial officers' personal private credit score and net worth could be affected by their financial decisions (just like citizens at home) some of these excesses might be mitigated. If you can derive private benefit from public dealings, then, in order to keep you honest, you should also incur private financial consequence along with possible civil and criminal punishment.

Proposition Three: *Corporations should not be considered persons and should not have the attendant rights of citizens.* This mistaken corporate "right" was based on court decision at a time in the country's history when corporate robber barons basically ran the government. It was a nonsensical decision, allowing for a raft of abuses, and should be vacated.

Proposition Four: Bankruptcy laws should be restructured so that citizens who legitimately fail on the private level can get back on their feet. Two-thirds of personal bankruptcies result from divorce, job loss, or failure of health.

Well-considered attempts to start a business, for instance, aided by scrupulously examined lending, and personal investment should be encouraged and supported toward success, through training, tax incentives, etc. If the business goes under, the hit one takes should not swallow one's ability to simply live and provide for family.

Proposition Five: The "good life" should not be about retiring early with wealth gained from speculative investing, but rather investing time, talent, treasure, and trust in caring communities of exchange with "returns" in higher quality living and respected, honored retirement as an elder within the community. "Get rich quick" mentalities should be called out as simply an effort to elope with other people's money and leave them holding the bag.

Proposition Six: Quality should be emphasized and rewarded over quantity/volume. Currently the "maximum profit" meme that drives big business injects incentives to cut corners and think short term. This contributes to the practice of creating phantom assets, so one can appear to be increasing market share. It contributes to corporate leaders pulling gimmicks like buying back their own stock to inflate stock value.

This mentality reinforces the generation of transactions, just for the sake of transaction so one can deduct fees.

> *Quantity without any regard to quality or long-term impact is another way to say "mindless business, heedless of consequence."*

We need better quality focused on long-term profit, viability, and stability. This is sort of the "seventh generation" view of Native Americans applied to the modern economy.

Proposition Seven: Use microfinance as a model for good business. Microfinance, small loans to the working poor largely in developing countries, demonstrates the opening of the world market to a new class of entrepreneurs and a way to lift many millions of people out of poverty. After the tsunami hit Southeast Asia in 2004, microfinance provided significant, measurable benefits. (http://www.sciencedirect.com/science/article/pii/S0305750X11000568).

[Update 2013: Big business and national leaders are threatening to create another bubble around microfinance. There is a problem in more than a few developing countries where the so-called "standard of living" of the poor has risen, right along with serious indebtednesss.]

Microfinance also serves as a template for good financial practice to so-called developed countries:

- **Diversification** (many loans are given to many different people)

- **Low default** (2% or less, usually)

- **High stakeholdership** (lendees need the credit to run their lives and business; it is not expendable)

- **Cooperation** (group lending allows lendees can to cover each other and lower default rates)

- **Pro-social lending practices** (focus not just on absentee exploiters trying to wring every penny out of a business, but on clients and owners themselves providing real services and goods to maintain a modest income which is invested in family and community).

2
UNHINGED

When Concrete Reality No Longer Matters
to the Market (and What to Do About It)

We are moving by default from a material world to a non-material world of value. Real value (labor, goods, production) is being stripped to feed parasitic, illusory "value" that consumes but does not contribute (interest on debt, currency printing, counterfeit money, fraudulent financial instruments). In order to turn this around, we have to unmask this corrupting trend, understand how it operates, and determine what its effects are.

With this grounded understanding we can help transform material economy into non-material economy in its best sense—using material resources to "grow" creativity, innovation, learning, diversity, community, productivity, fulfillment. It is a sad commentary that I wrote this original essay in May 2010, and none of the "status quo" conditions I have identified have substantively changed. However, the alternatives I mention are beginning to gather momentum.

INTRODUCTION

Something profound has happened, obscured by all the concerns about economic details and speculation about whether we are in a "deep recession" or a "depression," a "nascent recovery" or a "W shaped" downturn.

> *We no longer have a global economic system that is tethered to concrete reality.*

Parasitic, amoral, slight-of-hand value shuffling (what I would call the "unreal economy") has effectively trumped the "real economy," the production and exchange of meaningful goods and services.

Worse, we've let it happen with our acquiescence, our hope that we can just ride this one out, and our denial of what we know intuitively to be true—pervasive fraud in the conduct of global financial business and massive counterfeiting in the establishment of value.

Here's where we are: We've allowed big banks and affiliated institutions to simply concoct fake wealth out of thin air, and we have legitimized and rewarded these concoctions with a massive transfer of real wealth to a very small but powerful segment of the population.

Collectively we continue to allow predatory lending, unregulated private financial bets backed by public taxpayer money, the siphoning of huge fees from financial transactions, and the debt cannibalization of once-productive companies by leveraged buy-out firms.

A global economy mediated by an acceptance of a standardized, reality-based rule of law and value between nations has given way to the shrouded anarchy of transnational banks as overriding powers driven by their own brand of anti-public "interest."

> *What constitutes value has migrated from actual value, based in something you earn and related to something you can actually concretely use, to "references to value," some number merely assigned to some financial instrument attached to some good or service somewhere removed several degrees from its source. Think "mortgage backed securities" where the actual deeds to properties are no longer even in the picture after extensive "packaging" and repackaging.*

This is all a fancy way of playing the age old game, externalize liabilities, internalize gains, but on an unprecedented and potentially cataclysmic scale. It has simply been pasted over by superficial coverage: Political coverage largely deals with the "horse race," personalities, gaffes, and likeability of candidates over actual policy. Financial coverage has concerned itself with a relentless boosterism, tea leaf reading, and a host of other trivialities while the structural rot goes unreported.

Abstractions like the "velocity of money," along with whitewashing indicators like trading volume are used to gauge the health of an economy without sorting out whether such indicators are attached to some productive, underlying activity or asset. This all serves to create a convenient smoke screen for moneyed interests, and progressively makes the "new normal" one that thrusts citizens deeper into debt servitude.

POST MORTEM AND REVIEW

A post mortem is in order. The elements of this worldwide con game are remarkably simple, not complex at all. Apparently you only need a few things to make a mockery of the entire global economic system, and big banks garnered these few important things through "regulatory capture":

1) Unregulated, unenforced rules (particularly for derivatives),
2) License to "mark to model" (assign your own values to your assets),
3) Ability to peg present value to irrational expected future returns (based on unlimited, exponential growth),
4) Infinite leverage (no effective requirements for reserve capital in unregulated "shadow" markets),
5) Massive size, so that a particular bank is "too big to fail," and
6) Non-transparency and non-accountability.

These things, combined with the moral, social, personal, and cultural approval of maximizing profit at any cost, incentivizes massive fraud and counterfeiting. How could this be otherwise, given the premises?

So here we have a system where you can 1) make up your own rules, 2) establish any value for any asset you choose, 3) inflate that value a hundred fold based on ostensible future value and returns, 4) leverage that inflated value another thousand or a million fold simply on your say-so, enough to buy up multi-billion dollar firms if you choose, 5) lean on taxpayer bailouts when you get into trouble, and 6) do this without any disclosure or accountability, all based upon a self-interested formula you concoct to enrich yourself.

This is less sin or malfeasance than just plain lunacy. Yet, this is what we have and what we have allowed to gain the upper hand.

Literally, following the same formula with a little "solid reputation" sprinkled on, I can value my cat's litter box at a million dollars, trade on its ostensible increased future value to skim myself a tidy sum in profit and transaction fees, leverage my "marked to model" value of that litter box, a million fold to buy up Chrysler. I can then loot Chrysler, stripping it of its real wealth and infrastructure, gut jobs, etc. for short term boosts to profits, and then walk away a billionaire.

I can give any reason or no reason at all for what I'm doing. I don't have to tell anyone a thing, and no one is going to come after me. If they do "come after me" it will be to lard me with hundreds of billions of dollars of taxpayer money to keep the national or global economy from collapsing.

Talk about throwing good money after bad. The most I can lose is my litter box and now that everyone has a stake in the con, they have every incentive to cover it up and make me whole, both to protect against their anxiety and their feelings they've been conned, and to maintain a functioning dysfunctional system.

THE HISTORICAL PROOF

Let me stress again: This is not mere "moral hazard;" this is sheer lunacy of the highest order. Moral hazard assumes a rational framework where the "good" (productivity, efficiency, etc.) is rewarded. We have currently already established as "rational" an irrational framework where outright, willful lying, theft, fraud, and counterfeiting are rewarded. The more parasitic and more inefficient I am in this framework, the more I make. The more I trade an asset back and forth, the more fees I get.

Even if those fees eclipse the entire value of the asset in question, I am "rationally" compelled to continue trading as long as someone else is paying. If I can inflate the value of my asset at will and pay Moody's or Standard and Poor's to give me a AAA rating who's going to know?

It is sobering to contemplate that the annual market for unregulated derivatives alone, has exceeded global assets at a total volume exceeding 600 *trillion* dollars (http://www.huffingtonpost.com/2013/02/14/wall-street-derivatives_n_2681610.html) and possibly more than a quadrillion dollars (1,000,000,000,000,000 or a million billion dollars) if you were to include undisclosed derivatives.

This so-called "notional" value is a kind of reference value that is not the same as asset value or market value. However, we do not know exactly how much is being charged to forge derivative contracts, though "hefty fees" is a reasonable assertion (http://thismatter.com/money/derivatives/derivatives.htm). Nor is it clear what is being put up as collateral to back the claims made in derivatives. With reference values this staggering it would not take much to create another crash. (http://moneymorning.com/2011/10/12/derivatives-the-600-trillion-time-bomb-thats-set-to-explode/)

Exhibit 1: The Private Equity Tax Loophole Scam

Joshua Kosman, author of *The Buyout of America: How Private Equity Will Cause the Next Great Credit Crisis* does a pretty good run-down on this scam on NPR's November 16, 2009 "Fresh Air" (http://www.npr.org/templates/transcript/transcript.php?storyId=120391729).

According to the transcript, private equity firms (the new name for "leveraged buyout firms") like the notorious Carlyle Group have purchased companies in a variety of industries and are now set to default on about a trillion dollars of their debts, close to the amount of default for the entire sub-prime mortgage market.

Taking advantage of cheap money and lax lending, private equity firms will likely bankrupt about half of the 3,100 companies they bought, which currently employ one in ten American workers, according to Kosman. Kosman estimates about 1.9 million jobs would be lost as a result.

[Update 2013: The dire predictions by Kosman seem to have been avoided for the moment. This may in part be due, however, to private equity's ability to use tax subsidies and more generous refinancing options to keep companies afloat while they continue to milk them for profit. (http://www.cepr.net/documents/publications/private-equity-2012-02.pdf) My horse sense tells me that private equity firms are adept at the same "extend and pretend" at which central banks have become so proficient. This will unravel in the coming years.]

By squeezing out workers, cutting research and development, private equity firms sell to each other at a massive short-term profit that devastates long-term viability. With the mattress industry, private equity firms bought Sealy, Simmons, and Serta.

They then, according to Kosman, proceeded to essentially fix market values between themselves raising prices while lowering quality and durability. This worked short term, until competitors like Tempur-pedic gained market share and left the overpriced junk offered by their hollowed-out leveraged companies on the shelves. Market share and profitability for Serta dropped below pre-takeover levels.

The same formula is used with hospitals and other industries. Take a productive company with some reputation and loyalty, trash it, counting on lag time for people to depart, and make off with loot when it crashes.

Incredibly, going back to our theme of the market being "unhinged" from concrete reality, these private equity firms purchase companies with debt.

Literally private equity firms put their fractional "money" down, and get the companies they are buying to take on the remainder of the debt!

Ostensibly, since interest is tax-deductible, the reasoning goes, tax savings for the company accepting the debt will outweigh the disadvantages of paying down the interest and taking on the risks. Of course, unsurprisingly, reality intercedes in a different direction. The scam is exposed. The equity firm walks away, and the company goes bankrupt. Many jobs are lost, and the whole country pays.

Exhibit 2: Fabricated Supply and Demand Scam: The Speculative Run-Up in Oil

Remember in the mid-2000's when the media kept falling over itself to explain why gas prices were unhinged from oil supply and unrelated to any impinging world and seasonal events.

Back then it was all explained away by mumbo-jumbo about the price of refining, and how certain refineries were off line. By 2007, the U.S. had begun a serious inquiry, with some settlements won for price fixing by retailers (the "bad apple strategy" that always leaves the big boys untouched), and, soon after, the prices settled down.

Again [in 2010] a new unexplained buoyancy in gas prices arises. This time commentators aren't even bothering to pretend it has any rational connection with supply and demand. Oil supplies are abundant, demand is down due to unemployed people staying home, and the summer driving season has yet to arrive. Instead prices are being "expectation driven" by speculators betting future upticks in the world economy, particularly China's, will increase demand for oil. (http://www.npr.org/templates/story/story.php?storyId=125790575).

The bitter irony of all this future possible value being more important than the present actual value is that this speculation could actually drive prices beyond the reach of people with less money now due to the poor economy and squash the very recovery that would give rise to legitimately higher prices in the future. Again, a certain kind of twisted, counterproductive logic is allowed to run the market without correction from present, concrete conditions.

Exhibit 3: The Double Whammy Scam: Profiting from Designed Failure and Placing Bets Backed by Counterfeit Value

A recent government suit alleges that Goldman Sachs colluded with a billionaire short seller, John Paulson, to defraud investors and "construct a package of mortgage linked derivatives designed to blow up" so Paulson could make a fortune.

Continuing from AP reporter, Bernard Condon's, article in the Washington Post, ("Does Goldman Case Tarnish Cassandras of the Crash," April 21, 2010) (original link non-operational: http://www.washingtonpost.com/wp-dyn/content/article/2010/04/21/AR2010042103944.html. A copy of the article can be viewed at: http://www.omaha.com/article/20100421/AP05/304219816/1003):

> So-called short sellers, like Paulson, profit when stocks, mortgages or other assets they bet against lose value. In other words, the game of guessing which way prices would go was allegedly rigged in this case. That sounds bad enough. But some Wall Street veterans say the real tarnish on our erstwhile housing heroes *is the package itself* - regardless of whether it was designed to fail. *By just linking to mortgages but not actually containing any,* the Paulson package and others marketed by banks upped bets on housing to *more than even the mortgages in existence*, making the overall losses much bigger now that boom has turned to bust.
>
> Normally short sellers add rationality to a runaway marketplace," says Charles Smith, who oversees $1 billion at Fort Pitt Capital Group. "But in this case they were adding rocket fuel to the fire." The fuel here is devilishly difficult to understand. Called synthetic collateralized debt obligations, *these packages contained a series of wagers* on whether thousands of homeowners would continue to pay their loans.

The key thing to grasp about them, and the part that explains how they magnified housing losses, is that *they don't actually own any mortgages and so aren't limited by the number of such loans. Instead, these investments merely make "reference" to real mortgages to determine which side of the wager wins.* (my emphases)

Did you catch that? This language confirms the divorce of concrete reality and the market: 1) "Linking to" mortgages but not containing any mortgages, 2) not actually owning any mortgages but being able to bet on them, 3) making "reference" to real mortgages to determine which side of the wager wins, 4) wagering bets not "limited" by material assets. The last point could theoretically involve an infinite number of bets and infinite returns on those bets.

This is well analyzed except for one point: The core of this dealing is deceptively simple, even if the instruments themselves are deliberately complex.

> *Industry bettors simply concoct counterfeit value by leveraging their own abstract, self-assigned-value assets among themselves in a ping-pong ascending scale beyond the value of the underlying concrete assets. The bet has both replaced and exceeded the thing it refers to. There is no "there" there.*

Real money is siphoned in fees from the "marks," the pension funds who are told they are investing in highly rated, stable instruments, and then the U.S. taxpayer is asked to take up trillions of dollars of real debt in order to cover a counterfeit, undisclosed bidding/betting war. Should I be able to make a "reference" to the Bank of England, or food, or oil, simply collect billions of real money if I bet right, and lose my never-there-to-begin-with counterfeit wealth if I don't?

Who is the "house" in this casino in which someone can wage a series of bets on assets that actually exceed the value of the assets themselves? It's always going to be the American [or international] taxpayer, the public, bailing out an unregulated, morally and financially reprehensible private market.

Profiteers actually make huge sums of money by destroying the world financially and environmentally, robbing it blind, and then sticking citizens with the check for any downside bets.

Now let's see why very little is currently being done to correct this.

ONE NASTY HANGOVER: CULTURAL CAPTURE, COMPLICITY, RAGE, AND WONDERING WHEN THE PERPS WILL WALK

As with any successful "mark" in a con, the initial reaction by the abused is shame and efforts to pretend a scam did not happen. With the American people there is also more than a trace of complicity. People got high on visions of unlimited wealth and got a taste of their skyrocketing "net worth," fictional and bubble-driven as it might have been.

Some even used their houses as ATM's. This stems from a creeping and cleverly warped version of the American Dream, that we all could get wealthy without working if we were lucky or clever enough.

In the orgy to get in on a "good thing," people didn't ask the serious question about whether this collusion was a morally, socially, and spiritually bad way to live your life, not to mention an abominable way to treat others and future generations.

> *It turns out the "good thing" is bad for everyone*
> *involved, even the crooks.*

People will begin to wake up to this as more jobs get lost and the fig leaves of fanfare-driven recovery fade into an uncomfortable reality— the United States and the world has been ripped off trillions of dollars, more than can be paid back even on the backs of overworking two-income families.

[Update 2013: *A June 2012 publication by the Federal Reserve shows the average family's net worth dropped 40% between 2007 and 2010.* This includes significant declines in income and employment. (http://money.cnn.com/2012/06/11/news/economy/fed-family-net-worth/index.htm)]

Rage is beginning to replace shame as the promises of recovery meeting the stubborn reality of high unemployment, frozen lending, plunging commercial and residential real estate, skyrocketing college tuition, and expensive oil.

> *People are beginning to wonder, "Where are the*
> *prosecutions; where is the accountability?"*

Why are citizens being counseled to liquidate their retirements to pay for their upside-down mortgages while corporations walk away from billion dollar real estate busts? Why is public money being used to bail out banks that engaged in purely private, unregulated betting?

Part of the answer is revealed in the case of Bradley Birkenfeld. Birkenfeld was an inside-the-inner-circle employee of the UBS, a Swiss Bank and one of the largest banks in the world. Swiss banks pride themselves on their "discretion" and privacy, a policy that allowed them to hide stolen Nazi wealth for decades.

So it's clear that we are only talking financial and not moral "discretion" when comes to the Swiss banking system. In fact, Swiss banks continue to be a haven for tax cheats, international arms dealers, and anyone looking to park their ill-gotten gains outside the prying eyes of international law. After counseling clients (including American politicians) how to divert their money into UBS to avoid taxes, and even acting as a "concierge" to buy expensive objects for clients, Birkenfeld finally blew the whistle on the operation.

In interviews on CBS's 60 minutes and Amy Goodman's "Democracy Now," Birkenfeld and his lawyer outlined the depth of the corruption. From the April 15th, 2010 Democracy Now interview with Stephen Kohn, Birkenfeld's lawyer:

> Nineteen thousand American millionaires and billionaires had these offshore accounts. You had to be very wealthy to set one of these up. The government created an amnesty program, so if you voluntarily turned yourself in, you escaped any prosecution and even public exposure. No one would even know who you were. On the other hand, to Mr. Birkenfeld, who didn't even have an account, Mr. Birkenfeld, who turned it in, he was sentenced to prison and was not offered immunity. So that's the dichotomy. (http://www.de-mocracynow.org/2010/4/15/ubs)

Dichotomy indeed. There existed in UBS tens of billions of dollars of hidden, tax-dodges for the American clients alone, and all those clients got was a slap on the wrist and more "discretion" around their identities from U.S. law enforcement? UBS itself was merely fined 780 million dollars and forced to give over its names, a drop in the bucket for its almost 2 trillion dollar holdings.

For all those wanting a progressive resurgence of the level playing field and the rule of law, there is little evidence of accountability to nourish one's desire for justice. Hopes for real top-down prosecution are fading, but is there another tack the public can take?

Conclusion: A Possible Silver Lining

How can a world-wide economy unhinged from concrete reality perhaps result in positive changes (after, no doubt, a lot of pain)? The answer is fairly brief. Part of the problem involves mooring our own notions of the good life to our material subsistence and/or success. The notion that living luxuriously equals the epitome of the good life has stunted our development and kept us infantilized, even with the many technological, artistic, social, and cultural advances we have made.

We still spend a vast majority of our time grinding out a living in so-so jobs that do not challenge us intellectually or creatively and that displace quality energy and time we could be spending with family, friends, community, and world.

We can make things, even necessities, cheaper than we ever have, yet we are spending more time working. In the 1990's and 2000's, productivity skyrocketed in the U.S., but real wages remained flat or declined. Now we see why. We have become debts serfs to financializers and market manipulators, who don't even bother having a material stake in the game.

> *We can see two things from this if we are prepared to mature: 1) The good life, and even the economy itself, do not have to be primarily tied to material existence, and 2) We can do most if not all the things for ourselves that "experts" are being paid to do.*

We can decide to rent or share housing and watch each other's kids. We can decide to drastically reduce our consumption, thus saving the environment and de-polluting our daily life. We can move our money to community banks, directly invest into microfinance, or lend to each other through "circle lending," cutting out the big banks and brokerages.

We can help each other fortify and maintain our health through community programs and "medical tourism", cutting out health insurance and medical industry parasites. We can set up or join intellectually and socially edifying cultural groups. In short we can exercise civil disobedience, refuse to be stooges, create our own spaces, and and recommit to spend time and energy where our true heart lies, free from the delusional temptations of a corporate-driven reason for life that has shown itself to be both conclusively abusive and unfulfilling.

In the end, they need us, and we don't need them. This is the only "this life" we are going to have. It's a lot more adventurous and enhancing to be a cultural creative then a debt slave. So, what are we waiting for?

3

FIGHTING AND WINNING WHEN THE MARKET HAS CANCER

How Unregulated Profit Cannibalizes the Economic Body and How Democratic Citizens Can Effectively Respond

As a citizen with a background in the biological sciences, I was struck by how identical the profiles of "growth" are between the present accelerating takeover of economic, government, and business "bodies" by financial interests and the rampant progression of cancer in human bodies. Cancer is not just a metaphor; it is an accurate medical description of our emerging economic situation. In fact this resemblance is so close, that even the solutions I suggest at the end of this article mirror our present conventional and alternative ways of treating cancer. Again, this article, written in June 2010, remains quite timely, because "extend and pretend" economic approaches are still delaying recognition and treatment of financial cancer.

INTRODUCTION

As tragic as it is to see late capitalism kill itself with self-destructive practices, it is positively gruesome to witness late capitalism ravenously eating itself by plundering pensions, Medicare and Social Security reserves, housing equity, and almost any other available concrete store of accumulated value.

Economic events of the last decade, have eerily echoed some of those same inadequate responses and ignored symptoms that one sees in a person with advanced cancer: neglect of early warning signals, hubris and overconfidence in the economy's ability to regulate itself and recover, unhealthy living (spending way over one's means in a way that defers debt and accumulates waste), and finally domination by private moneyed interest over the "DNA" of public life, over public governance and the public purse.

> *In steps, uncured physical cancer goes from being a parasite, to a predator, to a cannibal. The same is true with economic cancer.*

In its early stages economic cancer parasitically financializes the system and its victims, using debt to harvest increasing interest payments and hoard productivity gains. When that well runs dry, it acts as a predator by creating liar loans, phony derivatives, and private equity takeovers of productive companies to siphon profits and fees at an accelerated pace.

In the end economic cancer simply cannibalizes stored "financial nutrients" and assets by decimating pensions, retirement accounts, etc. with duplicitous labeling (i.e. rating junk investments as AAA), basically mixing completely fake wealth with real wealth.

We are in late stage economic cancer right now. The economic body cannot distinguish between the diseased (fake) cells and the healthy (real) ones. Phony instruments of value have grafted themselves into national economies (check Greece, Ireland, and Iceland, and more to come), personal stores of wealth, institutional pensions, and future taxpayer obligation to the tune of tens if not hundreds of *trillions* of dollars. (http://www.marketoracle.co.uk/Article19454.html)

So far we have buried evidence and smoothed over symptoms. What we need to do is acknowledge and account for the disease. Only then can sickness be addressed and a healthy response developed.

WHAT A HEALTHY SOCIETY REQUIRES, WHAT A SICK SOCIETY SUFFERS FROM

Healthy cells require healthy food—substantial, fresh, high fiber, low glycemic, low caloric, high-vitamin and mineral nourishment. Healthy cells serve the free enterprise "commerce" of the body by lending themselves productively to the responsive and smooth running of the larger body. Healthy cells add something and take only what they need to optimally contribute. Their "mission" is one of maintaining vitality of connection and quality of "experience" between individual cells and the social body.

Free enterprise, well understood and executed, analogously prizes productivity, quality of life, quality of goods and services, innovation and creativity, transformative learning, honest and diligent labors of love, and enjoyable and engaging relationships and experiences for its citizen members. These are functions that create health synergistically both for the smaller and the larger, a win-win.

The mission of cancerous economic organizations is to maximize profit, withdraw as much energy as possible, and give as little back as possible.

> *When "maximizing (financial) profit" is allowed to gain power without reference, balance, challenge, or duty, no other cherished capitalist principle can long endure.*

Free enterprise gets swallowed by monopoly (especially over life necessities like health care) because captive markets and price fixing will always bring more money than honesty, competition, and fairness (especially when people are mandated by law to patronize monopolies).

Customer service which is outsourced or downgraded will bring in higher quarterly profits by cutting costs, even as it undermines long-term viability by turning off clients and eliminating decent-paying jobs for potential consumers. Ironically, this course destroys the very system and people these cancerous organizations depend upon for their livelihoods, a lose-lose.

Physical cancer is caused by an alteration of the DNA. Look at how strikingly similar this description of cancer from Wikipedia aligns with what we are observing in our financial institutions (http://en.wikipedia.org/wiki/Cancer):

> Genetic abnormalities found in cancer typically affect two general classes of genes. Cancer-promoting **oncogenes** are typically activated in cancer cells, giving those cells new properties, such as *hyperactive growth and division, protection against programmed cell death, loss of respect for normal tissue boundaries, and the ability to become established in diverse tissue environments.* **Tumor suppressor genes** are then inactivated in cancer cells, resulting in the *loss of normal functions in those cells, such as accurate DNA replication, control over the cell cycle, orientation and adhesion within tissues, and interaction with protective cells* of the immune system (my emphases).

The current economic disease is caused by a core mutation in the DNA of capitalism, which is now consuming the rest of the system. Derivatives serve as oncogenes fueling "hyperactive growth." Political connections ensure that banks that deserve to die, according to the functioning rules of capitalism, remain standing. In fact, such banks have gotten even bigger as a result of the crisis, and they have become more deeply inserted in "diverse environments" (pensions, etc.). Deregulation serves to inactivate the tumor suppression defenses, overriding the normal productive functions of the economy.

Cancer cells display "uncontrolled growth," that is expansion beyond normal limits, in addition to capturing an ever-increasing share of body resources. In cancer, the lifeblood of the body is being controlled by pernicious "self-interested" elements, whether in the physical body or the economic body, and disease and possible death are the result.

Social "cancers" also result in moral degeneration: Cancerous social elements (economic, political, and cultural) metastasize from being immoral (against basic public rules of fairness and dignity) to amoral (believing themselves outside such rules) to anti-moral (anarchically asserting their own rules and forcing others to live by them).

Along these lines, high-rolling capitalist players, driven by a uncontrolled and unthinking mandate to "maximize profits" at any cost to others, have become increasingly bold in bypassing, subverting, or ignoring remaining regulation, transparency and accountability, taxes on gains, and reasonable caps to growth— basically any relevant limit or responsibility. They have also become more "creative" in establishing and passing off counterfeit markers of value as real.

Mechanisms for system renewal, maintenance, buffering, and repair are getting turned on their heads. Environmental and personal health, prohibitions against insider trading, concerns about quality, efforts to establish a "level playing field" or save money or defer gratification become vices, taking away from "opportunity."

Greed is becoming a virtue, just as obesity might be considered a sign of customer loyalty to fast-food industries. Real family and community values give way to politicized, corporate-friendly efforts to freeze or drop wages. Irresponsible borrowers sit rent-free in houses they bought but refuse to make payments on for months and even years (http://business.time.com/2010/06/01/the-free-rent-approach-when-homeowners-just-stop-paying-their-mortgages/), while the virtuous get to contend with inflated living expenses.

If you look at cancer cells under a microscope, they look bloated and misshapen. They do not contribute, and they suck energy from the body, the higher octane the fuel the better. Physical cancer loves processed sugar for this reason. Economic cancer agents love zero interest loans for this reason.

In order to succeed, maximum profit, like cancer, must mutate and co-opt its surroundings. No matter what argument can be made for expanding market for "green jobs" or pro-social goods, a more ruthless and effective short-term profit can always be made, in addition, by exploitation, fraud, and duplicity which siphons money and energy and discharges waste, risk, and liability. We need an effective analysis and response.

ANALYSIS: HOW THE CURRENT ECONOMIC CANCER OPERATES

The context

Permitted practices, including destructive ones, derive from culture and moral commitments. They do not simply sneak in and assault societies.

The first thing many world citizens need to recognize is their own historical complicity with today's events. Cancer, even that driven by genetics, requires a hospitable context to flourish. The generations that grew up after the Second World War provided just such a context for economic cancer by re-defining the good life as an entitlement driven by ability to own and consume.

Technological and production advances, elation from the end of the war, a burgeoning middle class, and self-sacrificing Depression Era parents desiring to heap the amenities they never enjoyed on to their children, all contributed to a sense of economic "prosperity" based in material accumulation and enjoyment.

Anything that could increase ability to spend, expand leisure, live lavishly, and enjoy convenience was myopically considered the American Dream. The commercials in the 1950's around car-buying and kitchen appliances serve as great reminder. This all happened in happy disconnection from the systemic and collective effects of these individual desires and decisions.

The motto was basically: Maximize, maximize, maximize. Whether it was corporate profits, union wages and benefits, or the square footage of suburban McMansions, good = more. Furthermore, people's sense of identity and self-worth became dependent upon this ethic. Maximum "growth" was the creed, along with a belief that possibilities for growth were infinite.

Forget that this was, is, and will always be a deluded and ultimately unhealthy assumption. Unreferenced growth for the sake of growth is exactly what cancer is. For it to be healthy, growth has to serve some productive, enhancing role, one that goes beyond momentary pleasure.

> *Who would cheer a physical fever that escalated in temperature past the body's breaking point? However, more than a few people were hailing the overheated bubble economies as evidence of a "new era" of unlimited wealth.*

Evolving mechanisms for cancer capital

Once this "maximum growth at all costs" context is established and citizens willingly participate, it is a near given that the mechanisms and "creativity" around unreferenced, maximum growth will proliferate and become increasingly audacious and extreme in the search for new frontiers.

Even if the physical limits of the "real," asset-based financial system are reached, "shadow banking" systems and "unreal" financial instruments (i.e. derivatives) are constructed to keep the expansion going, not only cannibalizing real assets but creating fake assets.

In 1999, with the fall of the Glass-Steagall Act, separating investment banking from traditional banking, the last pieces fell into place for a two-tiered system: Private parties could extract economic gains through unregulated betting on the market in a "shadow banking" system, on one hand, and be backed by FDIC guarantees, Federal Reserve policy, and bailouts by public taxpayers for losses, on the other.

> *There is perhaps no greater tenet to functioning capitalism than that which insists those who take risks both gain and lose on their merits. Without this, there is no need for merit or propriety, and there exists an open invitation to fraud.*

Zeus Yiamouyiannis, Ph.D. | *Fighting and Winning When the Market Has Cancer How Unregulated Profit Cannibalizes the Economic Body*

83

That core capitalist tenet was effectively abolished along with Glass-Steagall (http://en.wikipedia.org/wiki/Glass-Steagall_Act).

Once you allow a non-transparent, unaccountable, and unregulated system to be linked with the real economy and insured by real assets that aren't even owned by the offending institutions, you are giving yourself over to cancer capital.

Capital must have reference in real assets for it to have worth. Without an effective "real worth" reserve requirement, banks can simply manufacture value on their say-so, and trade the counterfeit value for real money. The cancer capital cannot be distinguished from the real.

Without limits or accountability, one incentivizes not only market manipulation, but market destruction and cannibalization for profit. What was most curious about the recent legal case involving Goldman Sachs and hedge fund trader and short seller John Paulson was that this case allegedly involved not only the deliberate engineering of investment portfolios to fail in order to make money from short selling them, but the placement of bets on assets that *far exceeded the value of the underlying assets.*

> *There is perhaps no greater evidence of concocted value than to have bets themselves be worth more than the underlying assets bet upon.*

Here are some of the more virulent recent cancer capital mechanisms:

Collateralized debt obligations (CDO's): Package unrelated debt instruments like bonds and mortgage-backed securities, into levels or "tranches" of return based on the creditworthiness of underlying debt *as estimated by the company selling them and without the buyer being able to access loan-level data* (no conflict of interest there!). (http://www.nytimes.com/2010/05/16/business/16gret.html)

Synthetic CDO's: Place bets (packaged as investment) for or against the debts owned by others. When you see the market about to collapse, partly through your own malfeasance, bet against the market to bolster your profits and stick some gullible pension manager with the worthless investment "opportunity" to profit from the collapsing "up side." (http://topics.nytimes.com/topics/reference/timestopics/subjects/c/collateralized-debt-obligations/index.html?inline=nyt-classifier)

Credit default swaps (CDS's): Unregulated insurance on default of debt, frequently backed by inadequate, phony, or over-leveraged so-called assets. Now apparently CDS's are backed by the full faith and credit of the U.S. taxpayer as long as you are a too-big-to-fail CDS monger like AIG.

Naked short selling: The practice of selling shares without owning them (yes, you heard right) and then purchasing them or delivering them for a different price. Obvious criticisms are legion: creating "phantom shares," market manipulation (artificially deflating demand and value by flooding the market with phony sells for a company), non-accountability (no security or personal stake, the fact that uncompleted transactions end in a "fail to deliver" rather than a meaningful obligation on the part of the seller). (http://en.wikipedia.org/wiki/Naked_short_selling)

Repo 105 (Repurchase Agreement): Covers up liquidity problems by booking collateral extended for a loan as a sale of assets and the received loan as proceeds. Assets are often purchased back days later. If this is done just before a quarterly report it can make the company look a lot more solvent and stable than it is. In the second quarter of 2008, Lehman Brothers used Repo 105 to move 50 billion dollars off its balance sheet. (http://www.npr.org/blogs/money/2010/03/repo_105_lehmans_accounting_gi.html)

High frequency trading (HFT): Sift through the marketplace in milliseconds with high powered computers and complex mathematical algorithms looking for securities priced too high or low because the market has not had time to respond. Then, buy and/or sell securities in an instant, guaranteeing a small profit. These profits add up when garnered with high frequency. (http://www.huffingtonpost.com/2010/05/15/secretive-speed-traders-i_n_577557.html)

Capital cancer mechanisms thrive on:

1) ***Unlimited zero interest money:*** Nothing like getting money from the Fed bank window for nothing and buying up treasuries for a guaranteed return of billions of dollars. Instant liquidity in a box. Just mix taxpayer blood and serve.

2) ***Empty calorie money movement:*** Much like physical cancer, capital cancer loves high octane injection and circulation of easy money in its system. If it does not get it the easy way, by duping unwitting investors, it will create it the slightly less easy way by creating crises that require bailouts. Lending for productive purposes, schmending. Small business viability is not our concern.

3) ***Non-productive trading:*** Who cares if trades seem to serve no useful purpose. They generate transaction fees, and fees mean profits.

4) ***Accountability dodges:*** Like an effective cancer, non-detection and non-disclosure is crucial followed by non-treatment (i.e. non-enforcement). "We have to make a system that will say and show anything we want it to."

5) ***Other people's money:*** Still think the Social Security System has not already been privatized through government debt? Still think pensions are safe? When one plays with other people's money and swaps it out for counterfeit cash or promissory notes and those people retire and seek medical care in overwhelming numbers, where is the real money going to come from? Can you say health care and retirement crisis?

6) ***Profitable ignorance:*** "No one could have possibly known this would happen!" I run the whole company, pride myself in my hands-on management style, get on the cover of Fortune magazine and reap obscene bonuses but when the fraud and misrepresentation piper comes calling, "I know nothing."

Respecting the healthy limits of material and financial growth

Environmentally and financially we have hit the limits of uncontrolled growth. Replacement population is leveling off or even declining in so-called developed countries. Wages are flat or falling in real terms. Debt instruments and financial vehicles are savaging what is left of pensions and public savings.

> *We have to face the music, whether we feel comfortable doing so or not. Cancerous economic side bets have exceeded the value of the assets they refer to. We cannot live on bets. We require healthy air, food, water, reasonable housing, and real health care to live.*

Like an exploded oil rig hemorrhaging in the Gulf of Mexico, we are waiting for a miracle to be produced in our financial crisis by the very people and mindsets that created it. This will not work. Our own initiative has been weakened by decades of disuse, but it is still latent, ready to be exercised. It is time for us as democratic citizens to commit ourselves to the task of transforming crisis into productive, pro-social opportunity.

This will require relinquishing our false dreams about unlimited material and financial growth. We see now that these dreams are both unreal and undesirable. We are destined for a much higher and far nobler purpose.

In agreeing to "feed the beast" of debt and non-productive economy we have had our happiness index go down, our working hours go up. Our time with family and community has suffered, and our individual time demands have skyrocketed. For a system that promised increased leisure, convenience, and fulfillment, the current system is a proven lie.

That is not a cause for pessimism but awakening. There is no tough choice here if we are simply willing to abandon our illusions. We are currently supporting a system that is not only personally, socially, and environmentally unsustainable but desperately unfulfilling and inhumane as well. We have much to gain by transforming our purposes and practices.

RESPONSE: HOW TO REGAIN PERSONAL AND SOCIAL HEALTH

Just as with the human body, any system, capitalism included, requires a regulatory system. However, that is only the backstop. At its core, good health requires much more than the absence of disease; it needs affirmative and proactive generation of quality and vitality in life.

It would be foolhardy to leave behind a well-preserved corpse and yet have lived a meaningless, self-consumed life. Democracy and its servant, capitalism, have presented us with an opportunity to transform in response to a formidable challenge. We need active, creative, caring, decisive, courageous citizens to take up this opportunity.

You don't negotiate or compromise with advanced economic cancer. You cut it out, starve it, and hit it with follow up treatments, while simultaneously strengthening natural, native defenses and responses.

In order to succeed, we must fully come to terms with the unhealthy and frequently vicious guises late capitalism has adopted, and we need to stop supplying these guises with energy.

Next, we need to conduct a thorough and honest examination about how our own quality and vitality of life and that of future generations has been both led astray and inhibited by an entitlement and consumption-based society. Only after waking up can we devise practices, which both dismantle the cancerous elements and build up the productive and sound elements of a good life.

It is time to take an integrated approach to the comprehensive problem facing us. As with physical cancer, it is first important to identify, biopsy, and surgically remove economic, social, and personal lifestyle tumors.

Next we clean up the vestiges and effects of the main cancer through economic radiation and chemotherapy (which may cause more than a little pain and trial). Simultaneously we employ "naturopathic" and holistic economic techniques to build up the foundation and strength of our economic body. All this is guided by new and evolving purposes, priorities, and technologies for our lives.

Economic surgery is accomplished by cutting out dependence on cancerous tissue. We can start to do this as citizens by what I offered in my last essay, "Unhinged: When Concrete Reality No Longer Matters to the Market (and What to Do About It)"

> We can decide to rent or share housing and watch each other's kids. We can decide to drastically reduce our consumption, thus saving the environment and de-polluting our daily life. We can move our money to community banks, directly invest into microfinance, or lend to each other through "circle lending," cutting out the big banks and brokerages. We can help each other fortify and maintain our health through community programs and "medical tourism", cutting out health insurance and medical industry parasites. We can set up or join intellectually, (creatively), and socially edifying cultural groups (cutting out Ticketmaster and the celebrity industry).

Economic radiation and chemotherapy treatment is accomplished through accountability. All the false money in the system must be tracked and extinguished. Complex financial vehicles (CDO's, CDS's, etc.) need to be exposed for what they are, counterfeit money, and their originators need to be criminally and civilly prosecuted.

Losses being held off the books, i.e. houses in default, need to be counted. "Marked to model" needs to be replaced by "marked to market" (or at least some reasonable baseline, i.e. inflation index, if

Zeus Yiamouyiannis, Ph.D. | *Fighting and Winning When the Market Has Cancer: How Unregulated Profit Cannibalizes the Economic Body*

89

one is worried about panic-driven depreciation below the reasonable value of assets). Big banks need to be broken up and have their investment activities divorced from lending and savings.

Naturopathic and holistic economic strengthening would involve direct re-investment in communities, small businesses, housing, credit unions, local banks, etc. with the proviso that this money goes to local, productive enterprises. This would not involve larding hundreds of billions of dollars on multinational financial corporations and begging them to extend credit.

Local food movements, farmer's markets, local currency and trade for services, would all help people meet their basic needs while strengthening rather than sucking from the lives of real people. This would also have the benefit of enhancing what I will describe in the next section as "intrinsic goods" and "relationship capital."

CONCLUSION: A NEW ECONOMY

What would it look like if we actually had an economy and society built around things that matter most to us? What should we do when we realize we have not only become debt serfs under an economy that is wantonly destroying itself, but that we have neglected the very central reasons for living our lives?

The present failing and corrupt notion of economy paradoxically encourages citizens to glut themselves on momentary, superficial pleasures while deferring the tough choices and deeper issues until later. What if we accepted the tough choices and deeper issues now as critical and creative challenges to spirited engagement with life?

What if we asked and pursued the foundational questions: "What is the economy and society meant to serve? What is most fulfilling and important in life?"

When asking these questions for themselves and their societies, most people offer answers like: health, family, community, friendship, love, learning, creativity, collaboration, liberty, new experiences, diversity, meaningful work, cultural enjoyment, literacy, curiosity, responsibility, spirituality, faith, and so forth.

If you ask those same people how much time, energy, and money they are spending enacting these practices, principles, and values, the answer would likely be (if it were honest), "Comparatively little."

"I'm too busy working to pay off my overinflated home mortgage. I'm too busy trying to make a killing in the stock market, housing market, etc. I'm too busy having my money 'work for me.' I'm too busy unwinding, watching TV after another grinding day at work. I'm too busy worrying about my cratering retirement savings."

> Aristotle said, "We are what we repeatedly do." He was right. Do we like what we repeatedly do? Do we like who we are as a result? If not, then we need to change what we do, and thus who we are in the world, to reflect our deeper personal sensibilities and commitments.

What would a society look like that facilitated this deeper looking and action? It would be a society that recognized "intrinsic goods" (non-material sources of value, meaning, and livelihood) versus merely extrinsic goods (the production, manipulation, refinement, and measurement of physical objects).

It would produce, affirm, and share emotional and interpersonal literacy, moral virtues, enjoyable and enlightening experiences, worthwhile learning, and it would reinforce humane and rigorous social and mental character through its educational, cultural, and economic systems. It would develop modes of exchange that recognized the value of unpaid work and other forms of application that contributed to social and personal health.

There would also be, in this new society, "relationship capital," beyond what we now call resource capital and human capital. Relationship capital, would be an additional currency created by the value-added social exchange of intrinsic goods.

We see this source of value operating in the popularity of "simplicity" movements, in consciousness groups, and in social choices as more and more people, young and old, trade down salary for what Richard Florida (author of *The Rise of the Creative Class*) calls "amenities." Amenities are essentially relationship capital "perks"-- pleasant work environment, friendly people, meaningful, pro-social work, and so on.

These are only a few broadly sketched ideas summarizing and forecasting possibilities that are already present in our world. It is clear that non-material sources of value are increasingly influencing rational behavior and concrete choices, in addition to aiding the search for meaning, integrity, and love. It will be up to us to translate these vague but intriguing possibilities into a new economy and a new way of being in the world.

II

TRANSFORMING ECONOMY

Understanding the Present
Challenges and Opportunities

SUMMARY

Transforming economy (def.):   Intentionally changing the focus and use of money from "taking" and spending (i.e. reinforcing social control, resource extraction, and consumerism) to "giving" and sharing (i.e. liberating talent, rewarding effort, and promoting connection, contribution, creativity, and production). Examples: Developing sustainable, democratic systems for financial administration; moving from a material to non-material basis for quality of life; moving from fragmented, individualized analysis toward interconnected, global understanding of consequences; transcending purely individual solutions to cultivate communities of effective practice.

Major points:

- Fraud is simply creating value from nothing and passing it off as something. Frauds interlink and grow upon each other.

- Currently, financial manipulation, destruction, and extortion gain more profit than value creation, creating perverse incentives.

- In accountable free market capitalism, overleveraged banks close their doors, their losses are eaten by bond and stockholders, their assets sold, and civil and criminal charges are filed against lawbreakers. This has not happened because accountability exposes the common fraud in the interlinked global system.

- Why should citizens who have no stake in private enterprises, who received no profits or dividends, who had nothing to do with creating private losses, be forced to pay for private losses? The only legitimate answer is, "They shouldn't." Period. Anything that does not acknowledge this tenet is not functioning capitalism, and if it is functioning capitalism it cannot violate this tenet.

[Update March 2013: The veil is coming off. Bank implosions in Cyprus concretely affirm that even guaranteed bank deposits are fair game for plunder. http://www.nytimes.com/2013/03/27/business/global/bailout-grows-riskier-as-cypriot-economy-stumbles.html?partner=rss&emc=rss]

- Consequence and having a personal stake in the game is critical. Practices like naked short selling to manipulate prices down or buying one's own stock to manipulate prices up distort the market by eliminating consequence and risk.

- In a system without received risk, there is only liability, profit, and power/access.

- In a lawless system the fundamentals will not apply. Anything that increases elite options and wealth will be supported, and anything that co-opts common people's wealth, labor, and choices will be pursued.

- Analyses that try to predict near term market moves based on Laffer curves, Elliot Waves, and historical cycles will almost definitely fail. We don't have a "new era", but we definitely have unprecedented coordinated global intervention against economic fundamentals.

- Savers and other uncaptured economic players tend to resist manipulation, but those living on credit will tolerate exploitation, because easy credit makes prices and debt abstract.

- "Austerity" is nothing more than the delusional efforts of a status quo to avoid the consequences of its own fraud and to profit evermore.

- Systemically, all debt that charges a percentage ("usury") originates in delusion. Debt grows exponentially indefinitely. Growth (income and otherwise) cannot. This leads to a widening gap where the fruits of productive growth devoted to interest payments increase until those fruits are entirely consumed.

- Overreach causes a breaking point. Debt creates scarcity, which stimulates fear, which drives manic competition, which favors opportunism, collusion, and concentrations of power, which translates to abuse, which results in a collapse of legitimacy for the economic system.

- Reality is the revenge of the gods.

- Coming to terms with financial reality will likely follow Kubler-Ross's five stages of grief: denial, anger, bargaining, depression, and acceptance. We are still in the bargaining stage.

Fundamental challenges:

- Disaster capitalism is being pursued full force. How can it be stopped?

- International financial events have challenged accepted norms of fairness, equality under the law, reason, and sovereignty. Is the status quo giving itself over to financial anarchy?

- With no effective reserve requirements, leverage limits, or accounting standards, institutions with power can simply make up any amount of value they choose. How can this be effectively addressed?

- How do you re-establish fundamentals in a lawless system? How do you revive upper-level accountability and rational response, when normal cause and effect have been actively suppressed?

- Consolidations and mergers have tended to create monopolies around formerly competitive consumer choices. This may maximize short-term corporate profit, but lower quality and increase consumer prices.

- There is a savings shortage. Savings provide an anchor for financial sanity and fundamentals against exploitation, debt slavery, and monetary tyranny.

- Profit once was an engine of savings and investment (producing). In the current global situation, most profit simply means wealth extraction (taking).

- Stores of wealth (hard assets) are being cannibalized to make up for the difference between plateauing or declining production and ever-growing debt.

- Since unregulated markets are non-transparent we won't be able to confirm their illusory value until those markets self-destruct.

Proactive alternatives:

- Recognize philosophically and practically that any democratic "good" (energy, creativity, intelligence) emerges and connects though us from the bottom up rather than from control imposed from the top-down.

- Pursue debt forgiveness.

- Conduct trade through locally-based paper currency backed by local goods, faith, and productivity.

- Transform the concept of "quality of life" from worth dominated by material wealth and monetized value toward worth emanating from non-material exchange and advocacy— learning, community solidarity, environmental sustainability, etc.

- Allow personal identity to be more motivated by shared service then heroic individualism. "I am a more fulfilled me by a more effective we."

- Support restorative justice. Promote giving to a community to correct a wrong or simply to contribute as a concerned citizen.

- "We will have turned the corner when contribution to our collective well-being is not seen as an obligation but an opportunity, and exploiting others is understood not as an opportunity but a crime."

- Identify fraud in all its forms, exercise civil disobedience toward fraud, and pursue counteroffensive commitments to moving money, time, and value to genuine, prosperous, health-affirming, financial institutions and practices.

4

THE BIG SQUEEZE

*Predicting the Effects of Savings Extortion
and Abuse of the Middle Class*

More citizens across the globe are getting an uneasy feeling that they are being exploited by remote, unaccountable forces. Most of these citizens don't have an organized frame to put recent changes into perspective, understand how they are being locked out of the process, and plan how they might respond. This chapter sets the table for the "middle stage" of understanding and action, by predicting how the trends identified in the previous chapters will play out.

What is happening? What are the effects likely to be? How can you prepare and take advantage of emerging knowledge for investment and for citizen initiatives. The 2013 updates I provide in this chapter affirm the predicted trends I first forecast in January 2011, when I wrote the original article for OfTwoMinds.com. Many are still playing themselves out. Other predictions have yet to play themselves out.

Fair warning: This is a tough chapter. If you get easily discouraged you may want to skip it. The short-term trends look bleak (i.e. real and extended economic hardship for more people, no accountability or even serious investigation of high-level financial fraudsters). However, as world citizens, we cannot afford to either look away or become depressed. Instead we have to prepare. This chapter will help you do that.

INTRODUCTION

By now it should be clear even to the most optimistic observer that the global financial system has given itself over to systemic lawlessness. Once international banks were effectively allowed to print their own money in an unregulated "shadow" system and have it redeemed full value by national taxpayers, the charade was over.

The only thing left, at this point, given the full cooperation of governments and an eerie worldwide non-enforcement of law, is for banks to savage and consume every concrete store of non-counterfeit productivity and asset value.

Not only have governments from China to the United States committed themselves to a chess game meant to eke out relative advantages on a sinking ship, but they have positively rewarded those who are speeding the collapse. A simple, cannibalistic economic rule now persists until a new system emerges:

> *Economic manipulation, destruction, and extortion are simply more profitable, far more profitable, than good old fashion value creation. Disaster capitalism will be pursued full force.*

Whether a country is communist or capitalist, authoritarian or marginally democratic, no longer matters. Citizens globally have been made the pawns of a universal financial Ponzi scheme lurching toward a precipitous end.

Who cares if this course ensures deepening debt, austerity, suffering, and shortages for the world? There's a buck to be made! Who cares if my own children will be choking on the pollution I spewed into the financial air and water system. I'm rich!

When morality, reason, and sovereignty collapse together, we are left with outright anarchy, in everything but name. This is a reality so uncomfortable that trillions of dollars more of citizen retirement savings and other assets are likely to be liquidated trying to finance the "lean times" and regain stability in the hopes of the promised upturn.

Act I: Oligarchy Becomes Anarchy

This anarchy and its suicidal impulse were brought to a head, but by no means started, with the collapse of Lehman Brothers and Bear Stearns. These crises did however confirm that the gatekeepers had become one and the same with the barbarians at the gate.

The same story kept repeating itself and was easily predicted by the news accounts of single "rogue" traders damaging storied banks in England (http://en.wikipedia.org/wiki/Nick_Leeson), France (http://en.wikipedia.org/wiki/Jerome_Kerviel), and other countries in the past decades: The techno-nouveau riche found vulnerabilities in the "civilized" corruption and racketeering of the establishment banks.

These vulnerabilities expanded and softened as banks adopted unfettered gambling as a way to produce huge profits. When gambling didn't pay, scapegoats were identified and jailed, the sins of the system were larded on those individuals, and nothing changed systemically.

Later, young guns armed with razor wits and high-powered computers saw that they could guarantee for themselves multi-billion dollar profits by not only betting on collapse but aiding and abetting (and even sometimes directly causing) a crash of the very banks they worked for or dealt with. Supported by a profit-by-any-means mentality, they simply took market manipulation to the next logical level, and a Pandora's box of financial ills was loosed on to the world.

Consider Lehman Brothers. As detailed in Danny Schecter's movie *Plunder,* Lehman Brothers was brought down by a spate of naked short selling simultaneously coupled with exotic very short-term anonymous short positions worth hundreds of millions of dollars.

One can conclude with high probability given the established dynamic that those who engineered this and profited enormously from it were former employees or colleagues of said employees who migrated to hedge funds.

These players were insider enough to be privy to accounting tricks and frauds, the Repo 105 scams and so forth, being perpetrated by Lehman Brothers. They knew that Lehman Brothers was hiding gargantuan losses and skating on an illusory margin, so they devised a way to push them off the cliff by naked short selling and entrepreneurially betting on their own success. Why not teach the old farts a thing or two about their own game and laugh all the way to the proverbial bank.

With the repeal of Glass-Steagall and the collapse of the walls between conventional banking, investment banking, investment rating systems, and government regulation, the financier class had completed its diabolical project, a fungible two-tiered economic system "unhinging" finances from concrete reality, productivity, and value creation.

On one hand, a shadow banking system has created hundreds of trillions of dollars of counterfeit wealth (http://www.oftwominds.com/journal08/zeus10a-08.html) through the construction and leveraging of derivatives and mark-to-model assets. This has been sold and exchanged for real assets, i.e. businesses and real estate.

In addition trillions of dollars more in real wealth have likely been siphoned off in transaction fees, bonuses, and profit taking. We don't know the full extent because these transactions are not publicly reported, regulated, or transparent.

Financial, criminal, and civil liabilities were, and are still being, avoided through regulatory and governmental capture. On the other hand, infiltrated real value assets are being simply taken over: foreclosed upon, reassigned, and used as guarantees for this colossal fraud. Shadow liabilities are being hidden or shifted on to taxpayers' bills.

Unsurprisingly, hedge funds like Magnetar (http://www.propublica.org/article/the-magnetar-trade-how-one-hedge-fund-helped-keep-the-housing-bubble-going) saw an opportunity to profit from this inequality under the law by lobbying banks to construct highly-rated junk investment portfolios and then betting against those portfolios many times over.

So you have the young amoral renegade side of the elite sparring with the crooked establishment side in what amounts to them as one big galactic video game. When they lose, they always have another life. When they win, they take home the money and the title. Someone else pays.

It has to be noted that there is no personal stake in this game. Naked short selling, for instance, is phantom selling, selling shares you don't actually own. Phantom buying, which is what is currently propping up the stock market, is using Fed-funneled money to buy up your own stocks.

Risk has been removed from the system. There is only liability, profit, and power. Those of power and size taking great "risks" can leverage those risks into an extortion demand: "take our liabilities off our books, allow us to valuate them for as much as we want, and/or hide them for as long as we like or we'll blow up the system." Governments, with the exception of Iceland, said, "Please, extorter, don't do that. We'll do anything you ask."

If free market capitalism existed and worked these banks would have been allowed to collapse, their losses eaten by bond and stock holders, and civil and criminal charges filed against institutions and individuals. However, to do so would have exposed the rot and common criminality in the interlinked global system.

Accountability would have indicted the people and connections behind the curtain, so the entire anarchic enterprise has to be covered up and its costs shifted to taxpayers, in a vicious downward cycle, which only accelerates rapaciousness and irrational incentives and punishes savings and responsibility.

Savings interest rates have been near zero for years, significantly lower than inflation. Unemployment is high and people are liquidating their assets to pay for their costs of living. In addition, their future earnings and children's savings and being charged in advance for the multi-trillion dollar malfeasance of banks. Pensions are being looted and/or liquidated along with other real assets.

> *The major U.S. banks, on the other hand, reported within quarters of the crash they created, that they were able to go through an entire quarter without a single losing trading day*

That is pretty easy to do when so-called toxic assets are offloaded to the Federal Reserve for 100 cents on the dollar and when *banks receive hundreds of billions of 0% interest rate money and turn around and buy Treasury bonds with 3% interest* (http://www.washingtonsblog.com/2011/01/government-says-no-to-helping-states-and-main-street-while-continuing-to-throw-trillions-at-the-giant-banks.html), "paying" taxpayers back with interest earned on the debt these same banks caused.

No violations are too egregious or too pervasive for the Department of Justice or the SEC to ignore, no infraction too obvious or ridiculous to be covered up.

- **Fraudclosure** (http://www.ritholtz.com/blog/2010/10/fraudclosure/): hundreds of thousands of mortgages being processed by robosigners, recorded and shifted around electronically, and their paper trails neglected or destroyed, contrary to even the most basic commerce and property laws. Not a single significant prosecution yet.

- **Exchanges** (http://www.marketoracle.co.uk/Article7059.html): selling shares in precious metals without even having close to the reserves in physical metal to back it up.

- **JP Morgan's "alleged" manipulation of the silver market** (http://www.zerohedge.com/article/whistleblower-exposes-jp-morgans-silver-manipulation-scheme).

- **Mortgage insurers simply not paying their obligations** (http://www.zerohedge.com/article/christopher-whalen-freddie-and-fannie-helped-create-epidemic-mortgage-fraud).

- **Verified cases of houses being "foreclosed" upon that were already bought with cash** (http://www.rawstory.com/rs/2010/10/06/jp-morgan-thug-breaks-home-foreclosed/).

- **Same property sold to different owners** (http://mortgage.ocregister.com/2010/09/16/their-home-was-sold-by-mistake-2/37004/).

- **Extorted "marked to model" FASB standards fraud**
  (http://dailybail.com/home/william-black-calls-on-fdic-to-seize-
  bank-of-america.html).

  [Update 2013: almost all these frauds continue to run full tilt
  or have escaped criminal prosecution. There are some private
  lawsuits that may gain traction in the coming years, but so far
  big financial interests have been able to successfully circle the
  wagons. However, the forces punching holes in their barricade
  have not gone away. This defense will break down. It's a matter
  of when, not if.]

With no effective reserve requirements, leverage limits, or accounting
standards, institutions with power can simply make up any amount
they choose. The above examples show how rampantly financial
institutions have evolved to claim and sell any property they choose,
and valuate and sell any instrument they conjure up.

Power is all about access, and evidence shows where the current
power resides. National governments in full collusion and cooperation
with gigantic international financial corporations, have opened the
floodgates of access to the "little people's" wealth through bailouts,
Fed policy, and quantitative easing.

Those same governments and corporations have clanged shut the
castle door of the financial elite by allowing them to establish the
value of their own assets and to concoct, rate, and sell almost any
financial asset or instrument with no accountability, transparency, or
enforcement of existing law.

Act II: Abused Fundamentals and Fake Markets: How it Plays Out

So we have a lawless system. What does this mean for citizens and investors? In the near term it means that the fundamentals will not apply. Anything that maintains or augments elite wealth and increases elite options will be supported, and anything that consumes or converts common people's wealth and labor and restricts their choices will be pursued.

Anything that reinforces accountability, rational response, or cause and effect will be actively suppressed. Forget reversion to the mean. One only has to observe where the respective value/wealth of each party resides and where it gets channeled to know what the market will do and where policy will go.

When the stock market should crash, it won't... until some time frame far longer than even the most generous fundamentals would dictate. I said as much to Charles Hugh Smith in an October 17, 2010 email entitled "Stealth Monetization Keeping Market Up With Stock Buybacks," and so far I have been right on the money:

> I've seen different parts of this puzzle in various articles, but here is why the stock market will remain artificially boosted until the mortgage fraud mess really gets cranked up. Just like [when] the Fed lends to banks at 0% interest as a way to funnel money back to purchasing low-interest T-bonds, creating an artificial demand [for the U.S. dollar] [guaranteeing] profit [for banks and] staunching the exodus of foreign money, so too can money be funneled through banks from the Fed to corporations who use it to buy their own stock, effecting the same scenario. I believe this is happening now, and will likely happen more if there is a QE2 [Quantiative Easing 2, second stage money printing by the Federal Reserve].

[Note: In 2013 this continues to persist through QE3 and beyond in global central bank policies that subsidize non-value by simply restructuring national debts like Greece's ("extend") and printing more money ("pretend").]

Corporations will love it, because CEOs know that stock increases, no matter how you get them, mean big bonuses. [T]hey will, if anything attempt to hyperaccelerate low-interest money flow into their books and on to the stock sales block. How long that charade can persist is anyone's guess, but if you can have insolvent, zombie banks making "profits," [and handing out a record 144 billion dollars in compensation, then it might take a while]. (http://www.businessinsider.com/wall-street-pay-record-144-billion-2010-10)

The more extreme the hubris, the more ridiculous the momentum, and the more spectacular the crash. These guys think they can defy gravity, and so far they have [been able to] with a lot of help. When the natural laws of finance kick in is anyone's guess, but I see (the Dow Index) as I originally predicted, to be 11,000 to 12,000 (un)til at least March (2011), a shakeup, and some panicked back door bailout to obscure the fundamentals again until September/October (of 2012).

These guys are too arrogant, too insulated, and too single-minded to do anything other than attempt to force the world into their boxes. At a certain point it will quit, but that only happens when things get very unmasked. The mortgage fraud cases are the key, but those will be stonewalled. These guys are tenacious because they are hanging by a thread of testosterone. Tick, tock.

[Note: In 2013, the clock is still ticking, and the mortgage cases have gone nowhere on the federal level, though some action is gaining traction in private lawsuits.]

Analyses that try to predict near term market moves based on Laffer curves, Elliot Waves, and historical cycles will almost definitely fail. We don't have a "new era", but we definitely have unprecedented coordinated global intervention dedicated almost solely to the fortunes of the top 1%.

That is the new rule that will govern until there is a serious breakdown. Warren Buffet got this insight after the financial crash in 2008. He knew the government was going to step in to save and subsidize the big banks so he swooped up their stocks, garnering himself a hefty tax break [and profit] in the process.

In the near term, independent shorters will be routinely and consistently routed through market manipulation and collusion between large corporations and their government policy clerks. JP Morgan allegedly manipulates the silver market for its own profit, but also does so to keep fiat currencies stronger.

Feeling they benefit, major world governments will refuse to prosecute and, indeed, actively collude for reasons of "monetary security." However, if you happen to be JP Morgan, holding massive short positions on silver, and you get challenged by a coordinated democratic effort to "crash JP Morgan, buy silver" (http://www.guardian.co.uk/commentisfree/2010/dec/02/jp-morgan-silver-short-selling-crash?INTCMP=SRCH), then you simply offload your short positions into unregulated institutions and buy up the copper market.

[Update 2013: I was absolutely on target with this prediction. Metal markets have successfully been suppressed, and there have been no prosecutions.]

Here are some of my predictions in line with this rich-get-richer-and-the-rest-of-us-pay near to medium-term trend:

- The stock market will remain artificially high, between 11,000 and 12,000 with possible dips (7,000 - 9,000) and spikes into the 14,000 - 16,000 range, before running into serious trouble in September/October 2011 (lower probability and acuteness) and/or September/October 2012 (much higher probability and acuteness).

  [Update 2013: The market did limp along in the 12,000 – 13,000 range for a couple of years, a little higher than I predicted, and is now cruising upward in 2013, without the support of fundamentals or accountability. The timeline has been deferred, but the consequences will not be avoided as other stressors come to bear, i.e. baby boomer retirement and liquidation of stocks.]

- Wages will remain flat or decline, unemployment and underemployment will remain high, and the power of labor will erode further as unions continue to throw their younger members under the bus to fund entitlements and benefits of their older members. Worldwide labor will be cheaper, providing a near term boost to corporate profits (counteracted eventually by buyer revolt).

  [Update 2013: This prediction remains true, as labor costs remain suppressed. Fewer jobs and more people looking for jobs will do that. Long-term unemployment and underemployment remains high. However, credit has not collapsed to the point of yet creating a buyer revolt. Look for that to happen in the coming years.]

- Sales numbers will disappoint indefinitely, making stocks of retail stores a very bad buy. Even the Wal-Marts will take a hit. People simply don't have the money even for cheap luxuries. Dollar stores on the other hand will continue to do very well because the provide soap, paper, spices, etc. for a very cheap price. In economics, it's called "substitution." To the middle class and working classes it's called "survival." This will not stop the GDP numbers from rising, being recalculated, and being manipulated with debt-fueled government spending.

[Update 2013: This prediction remains true. Retail buying has reached a plateau, because people no longer have easy credit nor as much income to throw into unnecessary purchases. Government figures continue to be manipulated.]

• The middle class will continue to stay away from the housing and stock markets in droves through a combination of low income, lack of trust, and just plain angry refusal. This, in addition to baby boomer liquidation for retirement will put serious pressure on the Dow. This will be mitigated somewhat by those same baby boomers accepting that they will be working at least part-time until they expire.

[Update 2013: The myth of home and stock ownership as the ticket to riches and luxurious retirement have been dashed and remain dashed. Many have held on to their stocks looking for a rebound and others feel forced to gamble with them given the negative return they get from saving their money in banks (with interest less than the rate of inflation).]

• Middle class purchasing power will continue to be eroded as costs of necessities (food, water, fuel, health care, etc.) rise by several factors above inflation, and durable middle class assets (housing, savings) deflate in value. The material American Dream will become a distant ideal.

[Update 2013: This remains true.]

• Scandals and finger pointing will erupt around the management of public pensions as it is discovered that pension managers have colluded with states and corporations to hide losses and true value of assets. CALPERS, the 200 billion dollar California public pension will be ruled effectively bankrupt, due to a combination of extravagant liabilities and collapsed high-return junk assets. Investment rating systems will, as a result, come under renewed scrutiny to no effect.

[Update 2013: Watch for this in the coming years.]

• Metal markets will continue to be suppressed, even as countries and wealthy individuals and organizations buy them up as a hedge. Monetizations of debt, currency devaluations, will continue unimpeded. Other commodities, like rice, will experience huge volatility leading to huge price swings and escalating social unrest and resentment as investor parasites try to accentuate these swings for their own profits.

[Update 2013: After huge bumps, silver to almost 50 dollars/ounce and gold to almost 2,000 dollars/ounce, they have both leveled off for an extended period, silver at around 30 dollars/ounce and gold at 1,600 – 1,700/ounce. Some are predicting a break out in this relative stability as global monetary policy unwinds. The timing will depend upon how much the illusion of global financial solvency can be extended.]

• There will be serious talk of and moves toward a world currency and global accounting standards to establish a level "playing field" and keep nations from trying to undercut each other's currency through trade policies and cooking their books. This will be treated with a combination of alarm (by libertarians) and derision (by progressives) as observers will joke that now governments are trying to "be consistent in the way they break the law and steal from their people."

[Update 2013: Watch for it... Once monetary policy does start to unwind, and individual countries cannot simply undercut each other's currencies to maintain growth and trade imbalances, then there will be a "very, big and important meeting of global leaders" and this topic will come up.]

THE ROLE OF SAVINGS

Why are savings so important? In short, savings are the Holy Grail. On the opportunism side, savings represent many trillions of dollars of stored wealth, just ripe for the plundering. On the supervisory side, savings are the last reality hedge. Savings provide the annoying anchor for financial sanity and fundamentals, and serve as a barrier to exploitation, outright debt bondage, and monetary tyranny.

I'm defining savings as any stored real, productive value: money in a savings account, paid-down house, gold, land, a business, etc. Savings have utility. Savings can be exchanged or used to purchase material needs and wants or make room for the non-material, experiential elements of the good life—time, leisure, education, travel. In order to make a financial coup complete, savings have to be rounded up and looted.

Meaningful, value-backed savings means autonomy and choice, and autonomy and choice represent power, ability resist, to "choose other" than what some financial power wants from you, your money, and your productivity.

Restricting consumer choice is absolutely essential to maximizing corporate profit, since low quality and high prices improve paper profits short-term. Savers and other uncaptured players resist this, but those living on credit will tolerate it, because easy credit tends to make prices abstract.

> *Without personal savings that can be maintained, stored, and accessed persons have no leverage in their own finances nor in their ability to "vote" as economic citizens. They become merely servants to debt.*

It appears prevailing powers will go to any length to prostitute themselves against any true price discovery that would reward savers. Reversion to the mean, trading volume, velocity of money, margin, etc. all mean nothing when you can simply spew out an infinite amount of counterfeit currency.

Along with this, it becomes almost impossible to assess and determine what is counterfeit because the official numbers, formulas, and information upon which accountability rests have been so distorted and obscured as to make value determination impossible (see calculation trends in employment numbers, inflation base line, etc.). Political pressures and decisions have simply caused a regauging of "undesirable" numbers to make it look like there is no problem.

Profit once was an engine of savings and investment, the grease of small business, entrepreneurialism, and a growing economy. In the current global situation most profit has simply come to mean parasitic wealth extraction.

> *If I can profit by debasing your savings or forcing my debts on to your books, and you accept it as necessary to keep the system you've invested in from collapsing, I can control you and your future opportunities.*

In short, I now possess your power as a citizen. This is why Thomas Jefferson was so clear about everyone owning property. One's own means of support is necessary if a corrupt government emerges. One must be capable of refusing participation, exercising civil disobedience, and creating supportive communities significantly immune to upper-level manipulation.

Historical economics are premised on observations of human behavior converted into "natural" laws and forces, given certain conditions. Those conditions are being actively and systematically subverted. We are now seeing human institutions and behavior operating as purely synthetic phenomena. There is no Adam Smith's "hidden hand," no collective rational self-interest, but rather devolution to leveraged control and power.

We have the worst of neo-liberal state welfare, mixed with neo-conservative corporate welfare—a state for the corporation, and the corporation for itself. Citizens are being treated simply as productivity and investment batteries, like some twisted adaptation of *The Matrix*. With no protection from law or market fundamentals canny rational responses can be checkmated.

Act III: The Quiet Rebellion: Civil Disobedience, Local Markets, and Debt Erasure

The collapse of elite authority and rise of democratic civil disobedience will come, but I think it will look very different than most expect. Given the tumultuous play-out of current conditions, one might imagine comprehensive, violent upheaval.

There *will* be widespread and numerous local and regional examples of violence, John Brown style uprisings, especially in the worst hit areas. However, the overall rebellion will be mostly "quiet," I believe. It is likely to commence as something far more sedate and private than a global public conflagration. Moreover, it will be driven more by practical recognition and necessity than by principle.

Eventually, organized creative resistance and alternatives will emerge, but they will stem from widespread exhaustion in both senses of the word as in "used up" (environmental resources gone, savings gone, pensions gone, employment gone, retirement gone, American Dream gone), and in terms of "fatigue". People will become too damn tired emotionally, physically, financially, and psychologically both to fight *and* to continue supporting a system that is sucking far more than it is providing.

The rebellion will start as individualistic refusal and grow into something more interconnected, social, and affirmative over time. People will in increasing numbers stop paying their taxes and their mortgages, refuse to buy (stocks, goods, etc.), decide to take their money out of banks, and so forth.

From an October 24, 2010 email to Charles Hugh Smith:

> [Citizen rebellion] will [start as] a kind of civil disobedience that looks like apathy and complacence, but will be actually closer to disconnection and non-cooperation, and subtle sabotage one finds at workplaces with intelligent, productive, but poorly treated employees.
>
> These employees know they are getting screwed. They know their bosses and owners are venal... They know they have no leverage to raise their wages, and that performance boosts on their parts will be rewarded with more exploitation and skimmed and highjacked productivity. So what will they do?
>
> "Okay, two can play that game." You abuse me and my productivity, [and] I'll make it look like I am doing everything I'm supposed to, but I'm actually taking what I can out of the company, from office supplies, to internet time doing other things, to, you name it.
>
> I think [strategic] mortgage defaults might follow this same pattern... The salt-of-the-earth types still have some integrity and desire to "do the right thing" but if doing so enables them to get screwed more and rewards vicious behavior, the new moral mandate with integrity is to do the conventionally moral "wrong" thing, so as to punish the evil-doers and to prevent self-abuse.

I described how this might evolve in another email to Charles Hugh Smith on October 13, 2010 in a post entitled "An Unintentional Prophecy" that further developed a response I made to Gonzalo Lira's well-known post on hyperinflation (http://gonzalolira.blogspot.com/2010/08/how-hyperinflation-will-happen.html) ...

I have long argued (and laid out in some frameworks) how we are being forced in an accelerated fashion to move value from a material (including gold, commodities, etc.) to a non-material basis of meaning. We have overcapacity technologically to produce food, but undercapacity to distribute it in a way the optimizes well-being rather than reinforcing misery. "Disconnected" profit acts like a cancer, hypercharging certain parts of the system and impoverishing other parts.

You cannot eat gold, nor even commodities that are not in your refrigerator or your pantry. What value do these have? Since the central states and their paymasters (the financial elites) will fail, what takes its place? Most of the scenarios offered are of a survivalist bent, but I see this as a myopic, constrained guess ... rather than an outflow of keen, intuitive grasp of the possibilities.

When Y2K came, the world did not end. When New York City blacked out, people milled around... rather than storming the grocery stores. Fact is, financial collapse will leave us to our own devices, and we will have to invent. We have some tools: local currency, barter, microfinance, in which productivity can be linked back to (locally driven, globally linked) economic enterprise... [R]eal quality of life can emerge as present–and people-directed, rather than future–and "disconnected profit"-directed...

Connected profit, in conjunction with people and planet (triple bottom line) can be transformed into a quality-of-life value-added marker, rather than a power grab and concentration.

> *We are coming to the big face-off between top-down control by those who would be gods over us and impose value on us, and bottom up creativity which recognizes that any "god" (energy, good, intelligence) comes up through us and is connected between us.*

It is this "within" and "between" well-negotiated and exchanged that produces real value.

We are reaching the limits of physical exploitation and growth (as shown by its effects on environmental health). We need to transfer that growth and "frontier" mentality to non-scarce, non-material assets like learning, intellect, culture, music, community, family, creativity, human connection and interest. This cannot happen until the grip of the former is dashed by its own means, by its own unraveling. This is now happening.

This may look like pure idealism to some and capitulation to those observers needing cathartic overturn of the old system, but it will be in reality the acceptance of the death of an era, and the start of an open and creative building of the next.

> *Quality of life must migrate by practical necessity from worth determined by material wealth and monetized value toward worth in which non-material harbingers of value— learning, community solidarity, multicultural experience and exchange, environmental advocacy, etc— become the mainstays of a good life.*

Those websites talking about purely individual responses to catastrophe, for instance, those suggesting stocking up on physical silver and gold, and using it to trade for your necessities, will ultimately look foolish.

How will this solve the systemic problem? What merchant will accept on faith that what you hold is real? Your "silver" ingot could simply be coated zinc. Is that grocer going to take out a test kit and a drill?

Trading will be done in currency, but mainly locally based paper currency backed by local goods, faith, and productivity. Medium-sized cities (like a Madison, WI or an Ithaca, NY) near farmland and colleges with a well-educated progressive populace, farmer's markets, and a vitally functioning social infrastructure and comity will probably do best.

This movement will be driven by the younger, Generation X and millennial generations. Educated, well supported, idealistic, pragmatic, socially and multiculturally experienced, (and with lots of time on their hands) they face a world in which they have few to no job opportunities, huge debts, deteriorated expectations, a polluted future, and increased burdens to take care of the older generations. They don't believe the promises of future return they've been sold, nor should they.

In addition they are increasingly multi-ethnic, multi-cultural, and global in perspective, less motivated or swayed by nationalistic or racist tensions. Their loyalties are more to their own interconnected experience than brands, flags, or castes. They are smart as a group and very able to work collaboratively and effectively as seen in their impressive participation in the Obama campaign (before Obama completely dismissed them).

Baby boomers may follow, but probably only after initially resisting, and trying to make the system work long enough so they can cash in their corporate 401(k)s and extract their welfare state entitlements. Right now, baby boomers' identity is more deeply motivated by heroic individualism than shared service.

The boomers' deep-rooted hope for the material American Dream is likely to extend the time line for a global coming-to-terms with an obsolete system, but eventually they will have capitulate, find a renewed purpose, dust off their 60's idealism, and reapply themselves.

On a grand scale the only way to erase counterfeit money and phony assets valued at hundreds of trillions of dollars is to erase the debts associated with those *fake* assets. (Let me underscore again, these are not "toxic" assets, they are fake assets.) One way or another, this will have to happen.

What about those homeowners who bought more than they could afford, will they get off scot-free? The answer is, "not entirely," though full responsibility and accountability is likely to take on a new face.

Zeal for imprisonment of the fraudsters and the comeuppance of the loose spenders will likely yield to a requirement for defrauders and debtors to return fully what they have taken plus interest through financial compensation and in-kind pro-social work (not pennies on the dollars like the present situation). Though this would not exactly involve breaking rocks with a sledgehammer, it would help build up an infrastructure badly in need to renovation.

Forgiveness in general, and forgiveness of debt in particular, stand as virtues if they free us up to acknowledge, address, and learn from our culpability, start anew, and create forward.

There will still be a necessity for systems of prosecution and restorative justice to prevent abuse. However, giving to society, whether to correct a wrong or to simply contribute as a concerned citizen should not be viewed as a punishment. It can, and should, be seen both as a social necessity and a personal avenue for fulfillment.

We will have turned the corner when contribution to our collective well-being is not seen as an obligation but an opportunity, and exploiting others is understood not as an opportunity but a crime.

5
ENDGAME

When Debt is Fraud, Debt Forgiveness is the Last and Only Remedy

Finally we are getting to the turnaround, the hopeful future. This article's original August 2011 version received an estimated 100,000+ reads (over 29,000+ on one website alone, Zero Hedge) and was reproduced on scores of blogs. It led to an interview on the Keiser Report (http://www.youtube.com/watch?v=MGmayjY-QpB8#t=12m58s). Again, the necessity of debt forgiveness given a mathematically unworkable level of debt world-wide is still being ignored in favor of "extend and pretend". So this article is still ahead of its time in describing the likely arc of resolution as debt recognition finally catches up with reality.

INTRODUCTION

Finally serious economists are considering a position I have been maintaining and writing about since the 2008 financial meltdown. Whatever its name—erasure, repudiation, abolishment, cancellation, jubilee—debt forgiveness will have to eventually emerge forefront in global efforts to solve an ongoing systemic financial crisis.

> On a grand scale the only way to erase counterfeit money and (counterfeit) assets of hundreds of trillions of dollars is to erase the debts associated with those fake assets. (Let me underscore again, these are not "toxic" assets, they are fake assets.)... Forgiveness in general, and forgiveness of debt in particular, stand as virtues if they free us up to acknowledge, address, and learn from our culpability, start anew, and create forward." (http://www.oftwominds.com/blogjan11/Zeus-three01-11.html)

Debt forgiveness, therefore, accomplishes two important things. It eliminates the increasing and outsized portion of productive enterprise to pay off unproductive obligations, and it clears the ground for new opportunities, new thinking, invention, and entrepreneurialism. This is why the ability to declare bankruptcy is so essential in the pursuit of both happiness and innovation.

*Currently we are mired in a "new normal" and calls for
"austerity" which are nothing more than the delusional
efforts of a status quo to avoid the consequences of its
own error and fraud and to profit evermore.*

So bedazzled by the false wealth created by debt multiplication and its concomitant fantasy of ever-higher returns, this status quo continues to be stupidly amazed that people are not spending and that the economy is not picking up. But how could it be otherwise?

*Productive wealth has been trapped in a web of parasitic
theft, counterfeiting, liability evasion, non-regulation,
and prosecutorial non-accountability. All the fundamental
attributes of a functioning exchange economy have been
warped to reward creative criminals.*

THE UNSUSTAINABLE NATURE OF DEBT

Two observations: 1) Fabricated/parasitic so-called "wealth" destroys value and by diluting the value of productive wealth. 2) Debt/credit that cannot be paid back is never an asset and is always a hot-potato liability (needing to be foisted to a greater fool to garner "profit" and transaction fees):

> The models [modern debt are] based upon had no contact with reality. They assumed unlimited growth and ability to pay. When matched against the reality of people paying ten times their salary for mortgages that actually added more money owed to their principal (i.e. with negative amortization), required no money down, and set up "balloon payments," large step-ups in payments after a few years) there is no possible way they could NOT default in a predictable span of time." (http://www.oftwominds.com/journal08/zeus10a-08.html)

Systemically, all debt that charges a percentage ("usury") originates in delusion. Debt grows exponentially indefinitely, growth (income and otherwise) cannot. This leads to a widening condition where the fruits of productive "growth" devoted to interest payments increase until those fruits are entirely consumed (http://www.georgewashington2.blogspot.com/2010/10/michael-hudson-debt-grows-exponentially.html).

Once this happens, stores of wealth (hard assets) begin to be cannibalized to make up for the difference. You see this in Greece with its sale of public assets to private companies, and in middle-class America where people are liquidating retirement accounts to pay for their cost of living.

This problem is compounded by a private Federal Reserve that lends money into circulation at interest, and then allows the multiplication of this consumer debt-money liability through fractional reserve banking.

The money in circulation today could pay only a small fraction of the total private and public debt. That fact alone is evidence of a kind of systemic fraud. "If you just work hard enough, save, and make sensible decisions, you can get out of debt" could only physically work for a bare fraction of the population, given the money-to-debt ratio. The rest would have to simply default to clear the boards.

This is why debt forgiveness makes not only moral but rational, mathematical sense. Finances require balancing to be coherent. There must be some way to redress systemic imbalance. One has to be able to "zero the scales" to get an accurate weight of value and to re-establish healthy value creation.

VOICES IN THE DEBATE

Some analysts are beginning to see the forest through the trees in terms of debt forgiveness. Steve Keen, Australian economist and current deflationist, and Michael Hudson, American economic contrarian and prescient essayist, are both using clear-sighted reality-based financial analysis to debunk accounting games that obscure the untenable debt situation and to call for debt forgiveness.

How *can* selling sovereign assets and imposing austerity on Greek citizens (taking money *out* of their hands through higher taxes and lower benefits) do anything other than hollow out value and contract the Greek economy in the face of a deep global recession? Michael Hudson: It can't. Greece's debt needs to be written off.

> It seems unreasonable and unrealistic to expect that large sectors of the New European population can be made subject to salary garnishment throughout their lives, reducing them to a lifetime of debt peonage... (T)he only way to resolve it is to negotiate a debt write-off..." (http://www.globalresearch.ca/index.php?context=va&aid=18545 via http://www.washingtonsblog.com/2011/07/economics-professor-well-have-never.html)

Why isn't "quantitative easing" and flooding the U.S. economy with debt-money working to prime borrowing and lending? Steve Keen: Because the money is going into deleveraging in a time of overextension:

> Bernanke is throwing (a) trillion dollars into the system. Rather than that leading to ten trillion dollars of additional credit money, creating the inflation people are expecting, that trillion dollars is all that goes in, and people deleveraging actually reduce their level of spending by more than a trillion dollars by trying to pay their debt down, and it cancels out what the government is trying to do... We need a 21st century jubilee." (http://youtu.be/VoqaMzBK4pc via http://www.washingtonsblog.com/2011/07/economics-professor-well-have-never.html)

Other well-known commentators are not seeing the debt forest at all. In their contentious debates over deflation and inflation, neither Rick Ackerman nor Gonzalo Lira seem to be aware of the overwhelmingly fraudulent nature of present global debt– including the 600 to 1,000 trillion dollars of fabricated notional wealth represented by the derivatives markets, fraudclosure, and a host of other sources.

> Rick Ackerman: "'Ultimately, every penny of every debt must be paid — if not by the borrower, then by the lender.' Inflationists and deflationists implicitly agree on this point... and we differ only on the question of who, borrower or lender, will take the hit." (http://www.rickackerman.com/2011/04/heres-why-hyperinflationist-lira-is-wrong/)

I posted a pithy response in the comment section:

> Both Rick and Gonzalo left out the obvious third way— debt forgiveness. No... debt does not have to be paid by someone; it can be absolved, especially debt created upon fraudulent and/ or counterfeit-ridden practice... (D)erivatives are not real wealth, and neither was the ostensible climb in the values of housing resting in large part on those phony-wealth derivatives.
>
> The only "real wealth" here revolves around ability to produce real and needed goods (to allow us to survive), and the ability to create something that increases one's quality of life (to promote our thriving). Precious little of the present global economy involves either one of these. Yeah, if we use FASB standards and Goldman Sachs accounting, we can pretend our worthless junk is all really simply very rare, "unique condition" collectibles worth trillions of dollars.
>
> I've got a better idea. Take our financial junk out of the global attic in boxes, put them out on the front lawn, and see if anyone wants to pay a few bucks for the various items, give away the leftovers to anyone interested passing on the sidewalk, and recycle, donate, or dispose of the rest. It's a moving sale, and if our economy is going to get moving, maybe we ought to have one." (Zeus Yiamouyiannis April 6, 2011 at 4:11 pm http://www.rickackerman.com/2011/04/heres-why-hyperinflationist-lira-is-wrong/comment-page-1/)

HOW IT MIGHT PLAY OUT

This subtle debt extortion creates a system of never-ending debt-slavery for a vast majority of the population. When this "manageable" slavery is aggravated by a desire to use hardship to extort ever greater assets from the overburdened at ever cheaper prices (what Naomi Klein calls "disaster capitalism"), by open and unapologetic widespread fraud, and by the unjust offloading of risk and liability to taxpayers who had nothing to do with poor decisions of private banks, then the systemic abuse is revealed in the daily lives of citizens.

> *Debt creates scarcity, which stimulates fear, which drives manic competition, which favors opportunism, collusion, and concentrations of power, which translates to abuse, which results in a collapse of legitimacy for the economic system. Overreach causes a breaking point, and we are getting close to it.*

Will the response be warfare, taxpayer revolt, political upheaval, mass default, debt forgiveness, something else, some combination of all of these? I have predicted pockets of violence would be mixed with some softer combination of taxpayer revolt, mass default, political upheaval, and debt forgiveness, along with a return to community exchange to meet basic needs. (http://www.oftwominds.com/blogjan11/Zeus-three01-11.html)

This possibility of epic reprisal may very well compel banks to come to the table around debt forgiveness to avoid violent backlash and criminal prosecution, even over preserving their gravy train companies. Their assets rest on notional values, that, when unmasked, would drive big banks into immediate insolvency. They have simply been scam artists, producing little value and extracting mountains of money.

What might this look like? Looking at present trends and using the very useful framework of Kubler-Ross's stages of grief, it might go something like this...

Average debtor:

1) **Denial:** Liquidate savings to pay for over-priced house and cost of living.

2) **Anger and Fear:** Exhaust resources, experience want, compounded by austerity measures.

3) **Bargaining:** Attempt to negotiate with bank through HAMP and other mechanisms to lower payments. Banks don't bite and even have incentives to foreclose.

4) **Depression:** Lose/default on the house and move in with family or move to cheap rental.

5) **Acceptance:** Find out life is better without being a debt slave and spend more time with community and the ones you love.

Bankers:

1) **Denial:** Collect 144 billion dollars in compensation after financial collapse and not one trading day loss for zombie "too big to fail" banks completely subsidized by governments.

2) **Anger:** Express false righteousness, indignation, and hubris over toothless demands and regulations placed by governments. Exhibit sadistic glee at being able to simply claim and liquidate properties with no clear title.

3) **Bargaining:** Experience dawning awareness that "we may have just cooked our own gooses" as strategic defaults skyrocket, populist demands to prosecute fraudclosure gain traction, and quantitative easing ad infinitum dwindles and fails to keep stock prices artificially aloft. Improvise panicked attempts to "be reasonable" and actually negotiate, once the asset and money flow well runs dry.

4) *Depression:* Contemplate and realize possible bankruptcy by big banks. Retreat to the Hamptons to hire criminal defense lawyers, ponder empty life, and shoulder the abuse of media and contempt of a global citizenry.

5) *Acceptance:* Regain "good guy" status and avoid criminal prosecution by agreeing to be part of debt forgiveness.

Once defaults happen in increasing numbers and certain asset prices plunge (i.e. real estate), what will initially look like a bonanza for capitalist parasites could easily get out of hand, with people either unable or unwilling to buy inventory even at greatly reduced prices. Profits would tank at banks, liabilities would skyrocket even with most of it transferred to government guarantee.

Because no one plays the game anymore, banks could go under as well, as people rise to vote out bank-friendly politicians and simply refuse to pay.

> *This unraveling could easily force exposure of the notional value of derivatives in banks as worthless, meaning they are as bankrupt as the people they exploited. At this point, there will be a common desire and need to simply "forgive" the debts and try to find some way to distribute these empty homes.*

Conclusion

Debt forgiveness simply calls out either the inherent systemic inability to make good on debts or the recognition that debt was produced through fraudulent means. In the present situation, both conditions obtain. There has likely been no point in world history where debt forgiveness has been so comprehensively merited. The only speculation from my point (barring world-wide global feudalism and eternal debt slavery) is whether we will initiate such forgiveness or be forced into it.

6

MONEY FROM NOTHING

A Primer on Fake Wealth Creation
and its Implications

One of the great weapons of the financial system in defending itself against prosecution, accountability, regulation, and anything else that might imply responsibility, is its assertion that things are "too complex" to be understood by anyone but bankers. I debunk that myth in this essay. I explain in simple terms that the only "complexity" involved in "funny finance" relates to practices of deception and fraud that require one to pretend that value can be created out of nothing. This chapter should empower readers to confront the head-patting condescension they receive from so-called experts who are neck-deep in conflicts of interest.

> Only God can create... value out of nothing"—Justice Martin V. Mahoney in First National Bank of Montgomery vs. Jerome Daly.
>
> "(I'm) doing God's work." – Goldman Sachs CEO, Lloyd Blankfein

INTRODUCTION

What is fraud except creating "value" from nothing and passing it off as something?

Frauds interlink and grow upon each other. Our debt-based money system serves as the fraud foundation. In our debt-based money system, debt must grow in order to create money. Therefore, there is no way to pay off aggregate debt with available money. More money must be lent into the system to make the payments for old debts. This causes overall debt to expand as new money for actual people (vs. banks) always arrives at interest and compounds exponentially. This process is called financialization.

Financialization: The process of making money from nothing in which debt (i.e. poverty, lack) is paradoxically considered an asset (i.e. wealth, gain). In current financialized economies "wealth expansion" comes from the parasitic taxation of productivity in the form of interest on fiat lending. This interest over time consumes a greater and greater share of resources, assets, labor, and livelihood until nothing is left.

Only in a debt-based money system could debt be curiously cast as an asset. We've made "extend and pretend" a quaint phrase for a burgeoning market for financial lying and profiteering aimed toward preventing the collapse of a debt- (or lack-) based system that was already doomed by its initial design to collapse. This primer will detail the major components and basic evolution of fake wealth creation, accelerating debt expansion, hollowing out of the economy, and inevitable financial implosion.

STAGE ONE—FIAT MONEY ORIGINATION, MULTIPLICATION, AND DISTRIBUTION

The U.S. Federal Reserve System ("The Fed"): A private, non-transparent entity, formed in 1913, representing and serving private, profit-driven banks that creates money from nothing (fiat) and to which the U.S. government has delegated and effectively ceded its constitutional power to coin money.

The Fed essentially lends our "sovereign" public money to us at interest, paying for things like government debt with more debt, thus expanding debt. By contrast, the Fed currently gives away money to its constituent private banks at zero percent interest, allowing those banks to buy U.S. Treasury bonds, which yield a 2-3 percent interest mark-up to be paid by taxpayers, adding to citizen debt.

Fractional reserve: Private fiat fabrication of exchangeable public "money" as a bookkeeping entry through "multiplication" of public fiat held in private bank reserves. Holding 100,000 dollars of depositors' money may allow me, as a bank, to lend out 1,000,000 dollars. By what authority? None, really, just my say-so and my action.

In the court case referenced in the heading quote, Justice Mahoney ruled against a bank acting in conjunction with the Federal Reserve Bank of Minneapolis in its efforts to foreclose upon and "buy" a U.S. citizen's house by simply creating "the entire $14,000.00 foreclosure purchase in money or credit upon its own books by bookkeeping entry." Further, "Mr. Morgan (the plaintiff/bank representative) admitted that no United States Law or Statute existed which gave him the right to do this." (http://www.lawlibrary.state.mn.us/CreditRiver/1968-12-09judgmentanddecree.pdf)

STAGE TWO—DELUSIONAL, UNREGULATED VALUE ASSIGNMENT, MANIPULATION, AND EXPANSION

After money is created out of thin air, other market mechanisms have been propagated to magnify, funnel, and package value-from-nothing further still, creating financial vehicles that add more numbers without adding more value.

Leverage: The practice of arbitrarily multiplying one's alleged value in order to acquire controlling interest in another property. This mechanism is a favorite of now-discredited corporate raiders and leveraged buy-out firms that currently go under the euphemism "private equity firms". This claimed private equity can be a fictitious multiplication of self-assessed asset value used to buy a controlling interest in a productive company. Typically the acquired company is put into debt, its real assets hollowed out and harvested, and then the acquired company is allowed to go bankrupt thus making a killing for the raiders while destroying the ability of displaced workers to make a living. (http://www.oftwominds.com/blogmay10/market-unhinged-from-reality05-10.html).

Over the counter (OTC) derivatives: Purely unregulated, non-transparent, and malignant uncollateralized bets and hedges on market movements requiring no assets or stake in assets. Of the over 700 trillion dollars of "notional value" in disclosed OTC derivatives by International Bank of Settlements for 2011, the majority were supposedly "benign" interest rate and currency swaps, not the more toxic credit default swaps. However, it was a Goldman Sachs currency swap with "a fictitious exchange rate" that sunk Greece, nearly doubling its liability on just one deal from about 2.8 billion euros to over 5 billion euros. (http://www.washingtonsblog.com/2012/02/how-goldman-sachs-helped-corrupt-politicians-to-screw-the-greek-people.html) Also remember the undisclosed OTC derivatives market may easily be bigger than the disclosed market.

Rehypothecation: The process of recycling or using the same collateral with multiple deals and entities. Apparently England has no legal limit on how many times collateral can by rehypothecated (http://www.zerohedge.com/news/shadow-rehypothecation-infinte-leverage-and-why-breaking-tyrrany-ignorance-only-solution):

> Simply said: when one truly digs in, MF Global exposes the 2011 equivalent of the 2008 AIG: *virtually unlimited leverage via the shadow banking system, in which there are practically no hard assets backing the infinite layers of debt created above, and which when finally unwound, will create a cataclysmic collapse of all financial institutions, where every bank is daisy-chained to each other courtesy of multiple layers of "hypothecation, and re-hypothecation."* (http://www.zerohedge.com/news/why-uk-trail-mf-global-collapse-may-have-apocalyptic-consequences-eurozone-canadian-banks-jeffe)

*** Note: For concise explanation of the related mechanisms of collateralized debt obligations (CDO's), synthetic CDO's, credit default swaps (CDS's), naked short selling, and high frequency trading (HFT), see Chapter 5)

STAGE THREE—USURPING DEMOCRACIES AND CANNIBALIZING FUNCTIONING CAPITALISM

A cartel of international wealth counterfeiters have boldly made claims on Greece's national wealth through super-national entities like the European Central Bank. These claims are not backed by clear legal authority or logic, but they are being enforced anyway, administered by unelected technocrats and "agreed to" by complicit politicians acting against the interests of actual citizens.

Greece (with more countries to come) is being treated like a company town where "costs" (i.e. social services) are to be cut, debt servitude reinforced, and productivity milked through greater taxation. Corrupted capitalism continues thus to metastasize. Now that phantom paper profits are collapsing for the counterfeiters, real assets must be taken over to fill in the gaps.

Greece's national assets have been put up for sale endangering its national sovereignty and right to control its own property. Greek well-being is being diminished through austerity programs. This has only caused the economy to contract at an accelerating rate. *Seizing control of productive assets, and cannibalizing real wealth to feed counterfeit demands seem to be the primary unstated goals of these strategies* because the empirical results of these strategies clearly run counter to stated objectives.

Disaster capitalism: (http://en.wikipedia.org/wiki/The_Shock_ Doctrine) The intentional infliction of insecurity, suffering, and scarcity on a population to cause panic, compliance, and amenability to exploitation and extraction of wealth. It is a thoroughly vicious business model that operates in plain sight. When abuse no longer has to be organized and covered by conspiracy, one can confirm that capitalism's illness is in advanced stages. It is amazing how easily assets can be acquired and individual rights denied (as with fraudclosure) when people are overwhelmed by corruption on all sides.

STAGE FOUR—IMPLOSION OF THE BODY POLITIC OR NECESSARY TRANSFORMATION AND REDIRECTION?

This stage has yet to be fully entered, but the fraying of Greece's current social and political order sends a strong signal for the future of the wider world: Passivity equates with more abuse and exploitation, more austerity, and greater hijacking of national and personal assets. Active, civil resistance is necessary to stop the loss of public sovereignty to private interests. Creative, viable alternatives to the currently corrupt and fraud-ridden global economic system are vital. These alternatives and the implications of our current counterfeit wealth trajectory will be explored in the next section.

Implications:

The implications for this exponentially increasing dominance of fake wealth have only gotten more comprehensive and absurd since I last summarized them in 2010. (http://www.oftwominds.com/blogmay10/market-unhinged-from-reality05-10.html):

> Apparently you only need a few things to make a mockery of the entire global economic system, and big banks garnered these few important things through "regulatory capture":
>
> 1) Unregulated, unenforced rules (particularly for derivatives)
> 2) License to "mark to model" (assign your own values to your assets)
> 3) Ability to peg present value to irrational expected future returns (based on unlimited, exponential growth)
> 4) Infinite leverage (no effective requirements for reserve capital in unregulated "shadow" markets)
> 5) Massive size, so that the bank or company is "too big to fail"
> 6) Non-transparency and non-accountability.

So here we have a system where you can 1) make up your own rules, 2) establish any value for any asset you choose, 3) inflate that value a hundred fold based on ostensible future value and returns, 4) leverage that inflated value another thousand or a million fold simply on your say-so, enough to buy up multi-billion dollar firms if you choose, 5) lean on taxpayer bailouts when you get into trouble, and 6) do this without any disclosure or accountability, all based upon a self-interested formula you concoct to enrich yourself.

To this we can now add:

7) De facto take-over of national governance by private financial interests, meaning zero prosecution for large-scale control fraud, continuing complicity with and backdoor subsidies to big banks, and the stripping of national assets to pay for illegitimate debts.

8) Making uncertain the very notion of private property by allowing illegal and nonsensical assignment and title processes in the mortgage market.

9) Shameless annihilation of pensions and investor funds by simply leveraging those funds out of existence and charging enormous fees to do so.

How do we know this is going on? By looking at what is allowed to go on already, evaluating its profit potential, and multiplying those "market possibilities" by all the major players. If it can be done, and it maximizes profits (no matter how crazy from a systemic view), it will be done. The market for fraud is the most booming and has the highest profit potential. It pays far greater returns than any other market including precious metals.

Major players (Goldman Sachs, et. al) have the means, the motive, and the opportunity to expand the fraud market. In terms of brute gain they have been rewarded greatly (with no apparent downside) in cheating, hiding, conning, and now simply stealing. What do you expect they will do going forward? There is no moral hazard as far as they are concerned. It's all good for them.

Therefore, they will exercise no restraint. They will accept no self-imposed limit to their asymmetric destruction of broader functioning capitalism because greater destruction maximizes private profit. If anything, they will accelerate their demolition to get the greatest competitive share of what's left.

Look at MERS (Mortgage Electronic Registration System) and MF Global. They provide the clearest evidence of how the peddlers of phantom wealth will continue to push their anarchy toward social and economic breaking points. No action is too outrageous any more.

MERS: "Sure we helped 'get around' fees and recording requirements and seem to have 'lost track' of who owns what in terms of real estate properties, but don't blame us we are just a facilitator, a clearinghouse, an agent of transactions aimed at creating greater 'flexibility' in the mortgage market. Fraudclosure and those millions of forged documents attempting to retroactively record and assign titles, deeds, and transfers? Well, that is not our concern or our fault, though it is regrettable that nobody seems to know who owns what."

MERS provided an avenue for investment banks to slice and dice mortgages into "mortgage backed securities" (MBS). When you combine this capability with the advent of essentially unlimited leverage and rehypothecation, it is highly likely that the same real estate collateral has been pledged to a multitude of different investment portfolios. In not so many words, the same house has been sold to many different buyers.

Since there is no way to trace true ownership through the shroud of "complexity" enabled by MERS, railroaded foreclosure proceedings, and exotic securities, sweetheart deals get cut between banks and the government that, yet again, amount to a slap on the wrist, enablement of violence against property rights, and kicking of the can down the road.

When will the madness stop? When someone finally has to pay. Your guess is as good as mine on this, since the technologies of avoidance have become so creative and interlinked. I initially predicted some major movement in September/October of 2012 (http://www.oftwominds.com/blogjan11/Zeus-two01-11.html), but that has not happened, and we will have to see.

MF Global: "We don't know where 1.6 billion dollars of segregated accounts went." Poof, gone. And yet no prosecution, no investigation? What if your personal bank said that? What if your pension said that?

Yet, don't be surprised if you *do* hear this same "bewilderment" from Bank of America and CALPERS (California Public Employees' Retirement System). In order to meet increasing obligations pensions have moved to invest in the unbacked promises of toxic derivatives, so-called "high return" junk vehicles that were rated "AAA" by Moody's and Standard and Poor's.

> *As we speak California's public pension is insolvent, bankrupt. I guarantee it.*

In a classic Ponzi scheme it's current obligations are being met with contributions, and the so-called investments that have been made to fund future obligations will be exposed as empty shells when push comes to shove. The money will be "unavailable."

But don't worry, I'm sure the federal government will try to rescue California with "debt restructuring" or printed fiat currency. If the government can bail out banks to the tune of 700 billion dollars up front (and many trillions through the back door) why not throw a 250 billion dollar federal bailout to the world's tenth largest economy and one with the nation's most electoral votes?

Since unregulated shadow investment banking has been collapsed with regulated investment there are no guarantees that market values will be realized or that promised monies will materialize when needed. Almost every unregulated investment scheme seems to be following the same Bernie Madoff model.: A greater number of current contributors attracted by great (falsified) "returns on investments" are paying into an investment fund. Part of that contributor money is funneled to those currently liquidating their positions or requiring dividends.

The other parts go to fund financialized "churn": profit-taking by the managing company and fees (transaction, maintenance, representation, and processing fees, etc). The managing company then simply substitutes promissory notes for the incoming cash as money-equivalent "value" in their reports and in your accounts.

These promissory notes if inspected are likely based in nothing, backed by nothing, and answerable to nothing.

But since unregulated markets are non-transparent we won't be able to absolutely confirm their illusory value until those markets blow up in our faces.

We can look at patterns, though, and get a pretty good approximation of the scale of the theft. We can ask, "Where is the money coming from?" After the 2008 financial crash, Wall Street and its zombie banks were rewarding themselves with a near-record 144 billion dollars of compensation. If the money is not coming from them (since they just crashed), where is it coming from? It's almost certainly coming from us, and not just from taxpayer bailouts, but pensions, deposits, real estate, and any other hard asset or currency that can be scavenged and replaced with mere numbers.

What are more general implications of fraud building upon fraud?:

Ever-expanding debt: Lending money into circulation at interest in order to pay debt, creates more and more debt. The economy is forced to expand just to meet debt payments. Since there are limits to growth to real and productive economies, then unreal, parasitic, or shadow economies will grow to fill the void between skyrocketing debt obligations and normal production.

Unfunded social insurance, pension, and entitlement obligations: Population increases, coupled with a baby boomer population bubble, ballooning administrative bureaucracies, and governmental raiding of trusts (like social security) have catapulted costs and have stressed the medium to long-term capacity of social insurances, pensions, and entitlements past the breaking point even as delivery of services and funds are maintained for the short term.

Austerity measures will be coming sooner than we think to cover future obligations. Limited benefits, increased contributions, and delayed retirement are coming, but they will still be a better deal than junk "AAA" derivatives that disappear entirely once money has to be paid out.

Destabilized economies: The Fed's current policy of interest-free money to banks appears to encourage excessive private risk-taking, which is converted into public liability in the form of bailouts, thus further destabilizing the economy and increasing national debt.

Conclusion:

How can this widening gap between multiplied debt and productivity-backed money be reconciled? The short answer is, "It cannot." It is an inherently unsustainable system, where debt will eventually eclipse the entire value of all world resources, assets, and productive effort unless debt is simply forgiven at some point. (See my arguments for debt forgiveness in "Chapter 5: Endgame: When Debt is Fraud, Debt Forgiveness is the Last and Only Remedy";

original post: http://www.oftwominds.com/blogsept11/Zeus-debt-forgiveness-9-11.html).

We can also see we must come to terms with the unjust and completely unsustainable nature of debt-based money.

If fraud is something from nothing, then solutions to fraud involve re-establishing exchange systems based upon something from something. These systems are already being developed with local currency experiments, bartering, and a host of other emerging alternate economic models and practices (see "Chapter 9: Unleashing the Future: Advancing Prosperity Through Debt Forgiveness"). These options need to be expanded and further developed.

Our task is to identify fraud in all its forms, stop our participation in them, pursue a counteroffensive and commit to moving our money, time, and value to genuine, prosperous, health-affirming, financial commitments and practices. We can see increasingly that we have nothing to lose and much to gain not only in terms of financial stability but personal and community fulfillment.

7

THE FIRST
DOMINOES

Greece, Reality, and Cascading Default

Greece provides an excellent, ongoing case study in what happens when financial fraud by big banks continues to go unchecked and instead is supported and covered up by governmental central banks. This analysis was originally written in 2012, but continues to be ahead of its time. In 2013, the Greek economy is still spiraling downward and sputtering, while gathering a supporting cast from Italy, Portugal, Spain, and Ireland.

The conventional wisdom (sic) seems to be that the only way to protect a fragile economic systems ravaged by fraud is to subsidize and cover the fraud with the financial drugs of money printing and "restructured" debt. Having seen "economic cycles" before, central planners have convinced themselves they just need to tread water until "activity picks up" to magically take care of leftover liabilities. This won't work, of course, but if planners are clever enough, they can extend the time to defer discovery and payment of liabilities while deepening the economic pain of actual citizens.

[Update 2013: This has only been confirmed by recent data. (http://www.nytimes.com/2013/03/16/business/economy/seen-from-greece-great-depression-data-looks-good.html and http://www.nytimes.com/interactive/2013/03/15/business/after-five-years.html)]

INTRODUCTION

G reece is the epicenter of a drama that threatens to unwind with all the intrigue and subterfuge of ancient Greek myths and tragedies. As with the legend of Icarus, big, and now bigger, transnational banks provoked the gods with their wax-and-feather financial fabrications to create the appearance of soaring wealth. Now that they have flown too close to the sun and their wings have melted, these banks are being brought to earth by the obligations and consequences imposed by their fabrications.

Rather than take responsibility, these banks seek to appease the gods by sacrificing taxpayers. In fact, if one looks closely, these banks aspire to be gods themselves. They clothe themselves in their indispensability and shield themselves from accountability with tales about how many innocent citizens will be hurt if they don't get their next bailout. It is as if they say, "We are above the law... We are the law." Mathematics, legal enforcement, restraint, humility all must fall under the sword of their hubris.

In the end, just as with a Greek tragedy or a Yeats poem, this center cannot hold and things fall apart. When one abuses the laws and principles of mathematics and capitalism, claiming to be a faithful servant, consequence and accountability eventually catch up. The breaking point inexorably nears. Citizens are beginning to think, voice, and act: "We can do without the false idols that call themselves banks. In fact, we need them to be dissolved for us to survive and thrive."

Reality is the revenge of the gods.

NOT JUST ABOUT FAIRNESS: EVERYTHING UNWINDS

This is not just about fairness anymore; it is about the exposure of central, global illusions that affect everyone, not just banks. For the last three plus decades, debt-fueled "growth" has instilled a life sense that everyone gets rich, values always go up, and no one has to pay. If those illusions evaporate than those citizens complicit in this failed fantasy may actually join forces with the realists (those who knew it was a scam all along) to produce unified citizen revolt. Hell hath no fury like the people spurned and lied to, even if many had some responsibility in welcoming and fanning those lies.

The implicit deal was this: We will collude so everyone gets rich going forward. We will collude so no one has to pay if there is any unwinding. (But, hey, it's a new era, and that's not going to happen!)

Open default breaks the illusion,
and austerity breaks the collusion.

This is why default has to be hidden, deferred, restructured. It is not just about chaos around party/counterparty risk (in particular, cascading claims that are not backed by anything). It is not even just about finance. It's about all the other things that will unwind, culturally, politically, and psychologically, if Greece defaults and sets into motion the necessity of someone actually paying up. In short, recognition of reality has disastrous consequences for the status quo and its control myths.

The infinite growth meme unwinds: The cancerous economic obsession with infinite growth in a finite world is already unwinding, but will hit full force with cascading defaults. It is one thing to have a "slowdown," and another to have your economic brakes lock up on you and your gears slammed into reverse.

About the only thing that seems to be growing currently is the number of people partially employed or permanently unemployed. The situation is getting so pronounced that quality of life might actually have to replace quantity of possessions as the cultural indicator of the good life, and what would that do to the economy?

Politicians' power of the purse unwinds: Greek politicians, like many other politicians, will do almost anything to get re-elected. The easiest way to do this is to pay people off, particularly government workers and constituents, in the form of generous benefits or pet projects.

What happens if your tax base will not support this? You sell your political soul, defer, and/or hide the true costs of your largesse behind undisclosed derivative deals with Goldman Sachs that eventually put your entire country's sovereignty in jeopardy. As a result, Greece's former prime minister, George Papandreou, left after a very short term in favor of a unity government. Shady deals funded unsustainable perks that not only inflated popular expectations but created catastrophic debt and risk.

Guaranteed entitlements unwind: So now that the illusion of infinite growth is being exposed, the corresponding ballooning entitlements that enticed the larger public to become complicit in the illusion are becoming unglued. It would take almost a decade of gross national product to pay off the U.S. unfunded liabilities for Social Security, Medicare, and Medicaid, which exceed the staggering sum of 100 trillion dollars.

Retirement and health benefits cannot be paid out of fake prosperity and "notional" (i.e. imaginary) values. They require real services and products and an accepted public medium of exchange. (I will leave off the argument as to what constitutes "real" and "accepted" since even fiat currencies are dubious in this regard.) People will be forced to adjust their expectations and adapt their realities. With public and private pension plans also complicit in derivative scams to fund benefits, it will be no surprise if many pensions simply declare themselves bankrupt in the next decade.

The maximum profit mandate unwinds: We have reached such heights in our hysteria about growth and our psychological addiction to more-more-more, that we have seen stock prices *fall*, even with record revenues, if the corresponding company doesn't meet *expectations* of even higher growth and revenue.

It is getting to the point where a company cannot simply have a solid year and just pay out its dividends and maintain its good health. Instead companies have to be ever hopped-up on economic steroids and cost-cutting (i.e. shipping jobs to virtual slave labor in China) so as to not fall short of expectations.

These steroidal practices are destroying the companies and the means by which consumers can afford products and services. A relentless short-term focus serves no one in the end. "Maximum" less and less corresponds with "optimum," because present assets can be cannibalized or revaluated to give short-term boosts to numbers, creating medium- and long-term systemic and foundational deficits that destroy the health of a company and its surrounding society. Hopefully the idea and practice of optimum profit will replace maximum profit as the Great Unwinding continues.

THE CENTRAL QUESTION:

The central question, obscured by all the hand wringing and crocodile tears is simply this:

> *Why should public citizens who have no stake in private enterprises, who received no profits or dividends, who had nothing to do with creating losses, be forced to pay for private losses? The only legitimate answer is, "They shouldn't." Period.*
>
> *Anything that does not acknowledge this tenet is not functioning capitalism, and if it is functioning capitalism it cannot violate this tenet.*

Yet we witness apologist expert after expert excusing this fatal breach in capital practice as "regrettable but necessary to save the system." They seem not to have noticed that the system has already killed itself by violating its own foundational laws and principles. If anything, current conventional practice might be accurately described as an all-out anti-capitalist assault on democratic free enterprise.

> *"Why are we paying for something we did not buy and had no hand in creating?" The answer: We no longer have functioning capitalism.*

Call it what you want— corporate socialism, crony capitalism, cancer capitalism, plutocracy, kleptocracy, oligarchy, neofeudalism— the system we have now is the equivalent of Person A going up to a Complete Stranger B on the street and shaking that stranger down for "protection money" to pay for Person A's underwater house mortgage.

As this simple fact grips the population, and people wake up to the present economic reality, there will be increasingly organized moves toward civil disobedience and alternative economy. "Cannot pay" will merge with "will not pay" since the only way to re-establish health and integrity in a corrupted economic system is to starve the cancers that have taken it over. This has already started with Occupy Wall Street, strategic defaults, and riots in Greece.

So if someone asks you, seeking to appeal to your fear, self-interest, and need for approval, if you are willing to "be responsible for bringing down the global system," your answer should be an emphatic, "Yes." "Are you asking if I want to bring down fraud, theft, abuse and the cancer that global finance has become for me, my neighbors, my children, and my children's children? Are you asking me if I want to replace the current broken system with something that serves actual people? Not only, 'yes,' but 'heck, yes.'"

III
CONNECTED COMMUNITIES

Embracing the Future of
Democratic Capitalism

SUMMARY

Democratic capitalism (def.): "Having money serve people." A capital system of, by, and for the people that respects and elevates the broader rights, dignity, and well-being of world citizens over financial interests. A capital system that rewards social collaboration and personal productivity. A system of money exchange that increases citizens' connection, creativity, and contribution and promotes the healthy, fulfilling development of multiple talents, ideas, and values. Examples: Crowd funding, circle lending, community cooperatives, "triple bottom line" (people, planet, profit), local currency, car sharing, grass-roots initiatives.

Major points:

- Productivity means giving to the future rather than taking from the future.

- People do work. Money does not do work. "Don't work for a living. Let your money work for you," is based on a falsehood.

- Less greed = better capitalism. Greed weakens healthy, democratic capitalism.

- "Making a living" means creating life and adding to economies. "Making a killing" means taking life and sucking from economies.

- Free enterprise means opportunity to try a new venture, gain financial rewards for success, and receive learning and character-building experience from failure.

- Applied effort produces value, not smoke and mirrors.

- Stakeholdership means "invest money, contribute effort, and commit" rather than "take the money and run."

- Sound public money backed by the productive efforts of its citizens is the only real money. Privately constructed fiat currency is purely counterfeit money.

- When something seems to be too good to be true, it probably is. Quick and easy money almost always involves some kind of shortcut or abuse.

- Owners are ultimately stewards. Owners die. Properties persist. A property deed or lease does not confer the right to ruin that property for future generations.

- Ownership does not guarantee stability. In fact, the opposite often prevails.

- Social Security is insurance against poverty and disability, not a retirement plan.

- Values go down and not always up. Rhetoric that says otherwise is delusion.

- The living shall not be beholden to the dead in debts or in laws.

- Younger generations in greater numbers are beginning to value "use" over "thing," active experience and application over passive possession and status.

- The most irresponsible debt players by far have been those controlling our current debt system. Underwater mortgage holders are not the core problem.

- By a huge margin, our biggest global debt involves "borrowing" from Mother Nature in resource extraction, and "depositing" toxic pollution liabilities.

- Even responsible borrowers can go bankrupt due to unexpected events like health problems, divorce, or job loss. They cannot be expected to pay debt forever.

- Financial debt is not natural. It is created by humans and can be erased by humans.

- Capitalism stands and falls upon care, not the superficial "I-feel-your-pain" type, but the deep, committed "I-give-a-damn" type.

- "I give a damn" means: I get deeply involved, I refuse to ignore what is going on around me, and I confront and respond to challenge. "Give" is the operative word.

- Productive citizens are the ones producing the value. It is they who warrant financial decision-making authority, not freeloading financializers.

- *Having* money *never* makes you better than someone else. What is relevant is how you get your money. Any tool or crook can possess large sums of money.

- Real personal worth involves human character and choices. It is not a financial dollar figure.

- Maximizing personal profit at any cost destroys capitalism and capitalist societies. It is better to think in terms of an "optimum" profit that balances social tradeoffs.

- Profiting by countering irrational exuberance = okay. Profiteering off the misery of others = not okay.

Fundamental challenges:

- "Prosperity" has been reduced to getting your "goodies"—profits, entitlements, benefits, windfalls, special favors, and bonuses— whether they are earned or not and whether there is money for them or not.

- Most say they want free enterprise in a democratic market exchange economy that seeks to maximize responsible life engagement, enjoyment, and fulfillment. So how come we are currently stuck with the opposite?

- U.S. and global economies do not make any meaningful distinction between healthy and harmful growth. Economic sinkholes, like exotic derivatives or housing bubbles, are treated the same as healthy, expanding small businesses.

- Why aren't taxpayers, through government, gaining intellectual property rights and a capital stake in enterprises that monetize taxpayer-supported innovation and research and development?

- Irresponsible borrowing by past generations is being foisted on younger generations who neither decided upon nor benefited from that borrowing.

- How do you get a society based in individual heroism, status, and guarantee to evolve, when its addiction to image and security appears to prevent adaption, learning, and experimentation when the old approaches fail?

- How do you handle widening debt, especially when only a small fraction of the total worldwide debt could physically be paid off? What about the money-to-debt ratio, which is widening through fractional reserve lending and leveraging?

- Major global economies (United States, European Union, China, et. al.) are collectively insolvent and engaging in massive interactive fraud, misrepresentation of national financial health, and mutual exploitation.

- Non-democratic transnational corporations allied with so-called ruling elites in governments have superseded democratic sovereignty in the control of capital.

Proactive alternatives:

- Elect people to government with integrity, courage, and ability to collaborate.

- Redefine prosperity as being created from effort. Uphold this prosperity in the form of publicly supported productivity, ingenuity, diversity, and diligence.

- Make a clear distinction between productive activities and parasitic activities and use this distinction in the calculation of GDP.

- Incentivize giving and circulation of pro-social goods and services. Peg financial benefits of government workers to the nation's financial growth.

- Call out the fallacy of a war between personal and social interest. Fulfilling personal existence relies upon healthy relationships.

- Innovate incentives to invest for the productive long haul. For instance, give increasingly greater dividends per share (a loyalty premium) to people who have invested longer with a company. Develop local currencies to be used alongside national currencies.

- Have an independent, non-profit, multi-stakeholder agency setting monetary policy to help make sure that monetary policy is responsive, equitable, and more resistant to lobbying.

- Support peer-to-peer lending, circle lending, micro lending, crowd funding and other forms of financing that eliminate middlemen and reduce fees.

- Eliminate the Federal Reserve, print money directly from the Treasury, and democratize access of community banks and non-profits to low-interest national lending.

- Create "service swaps." "Hire" people who are unemployed but eager to be active. Create a currency exchange where debts, services, and surplus goods can be exchanged (perhaps with local currency) for this pro-social work.

- Re-establish transparent and accountable markets through better enforcement and stronger laws. Fully fund a sizable team of financial forensics experts to scour for signs of fraud or cover-up. Fire deregulation ideologues in regulatory positions.

- Constitutionally overturn inequitable, market-distorting laws like California's Proposition 13 (which artificially suppress taxes for some and increases them for others) as a violation of equal protection, equal treatment, and equal opportunity.

- Hit disaster capitalism hard. Have life necessities (water, air, housing, health care, electricity, etc.) be stewarded by the public and administered by cooperatives.

- Encourage giving over receiving by increasing tax advantages for donations.

- Eliminate guarantees on return for government contracts. Ban "cost-plus" accounting, no-bid contracts, etc.

- Establish single-payer health care, primarily administered by local cooperatives.

- Eliminate exemptions from anti-trust laws, be it baseball, health care, or big banks.

- Create competitive alternatives to the current monopolies of high-priced school lending and low-delivery higher education.

- Align debt repayment with "variable rate" economic productivity curves and contingencies instead of extracting more from the borrower regardless of context.

- Transfer money out of too-big-too-fail banks, all of it.

- Rebel against the consumerist "American Dream" that is making your life a nightmare.

- Say "no" to debt servitude! If you cannot pay your debt, seek legal, political, and personal solutions.

- Say "yes" to strengthening, simplifying, and de-expensing your life.

- Pool your money, resources, and time.

- Collaborate over employment. Share wages, work less, and volunteer more as a way to receive a living wage and to maximize non-material life benefits.

- Incorporate youth leadership and representation in high-level decision-making.

- Develop networked, resource-minded, creativity and entrepreneurialism. Co-invest with others in living arrangements, in job hiring, in crowd funding, in informing where one puts time, focus, and intention.

- Meritocracy 2.0: Emphasize social problem-solving and professional effectiveness over schmoozing and seniority in promotion assessments.

8

MAKING A LIVING VS. MAKING A KILLING

Creating a Healthy Democratic Foundation for Economies

These terms, "making a living" and "making a killing," sum up so much of our current economic schizophrenia. "Making a living" succinctly and perfectly describes the purposes of democratic capitalism, and "making a killing" encapsulates corrupted capitalism.

It is amazing how much of the general public against its own interest has literally "bought into" the "making a killing" framework. In this framework, you choose whatever maximizes individual gain, regardless of how many other people it injures. "Sweatshops? No problem, as long as the money is rolling in. Just don't tell me about them." If everybody chooses this, then we have collectively agreed to let the worst and most abusive and exploitative economic practices gain the upper hand.

Contrast this to "making a living." This concept does not mean "getting by." It means what it says, "making a life," and making economic decisions that enhance the life of self along with the well-being of others. This essay lays out the principles of making a living and presents numerous specific ways where "making a living" can become the rule rather than the exception.

Without a distinction between productive activities and parasitic activities there is no viable way forward economically. This three-part essay will begin to make those distinctions and provide recommendations on increasing healthy productive capacity and eliminating harmful parasitic activities.

Part 1: Introduction and basic principles:

> The current global financial unraveling and meltdown has brought us face-to-face with a stark and uncomfortable truth: with all its reassuring numbers, our financial system is a human system, based on human frailties and desires, resting almost completely upon imaginary notions of worth. Historical financial innovations have led us piece by piece into a phase shift from ownership of real assets to control

of concocted wealth that no longer has a credible authoritative connection to productivity, life needs, or the day-to-day requirements of commerce." (http://www.oftwominds.com/blogoct08/positives3-10-08.html)

I wrote this in October of 2008. Since then the only thing that seems to have changed is the intensity, complexity, and ferocity with which global agencies are trying to pretend and extend past our insolvent, incoherent, and fantasy-riddled global financial system. I continued:

> From the bartering of material goods and services, to the convenient exchange of dollars no longer backed by anything but faith, to "creative" financial vehicles that leverage essentially symbolic wealth to an infinite degree, we have progressively departed from the foundation of what was once considered financial worth—the competent stakeholdership, ownership, and stewardship of real property involving labor, earnings, investment, risk, reward, and responsibility. In other words, we've reached the "asymptote," the mathematical limit whereby even an infinite increase in concocted value produces no growth of worth on the real level." (http://www.oftwominds.com/blogoct08/positives3-10-08.html)

In this current essay I outline some possible ways to press onward from this stalemate with reality. In order to do so we must be willing to pierce economic illusions and to draw out the differences between what we claim we want and what our actions actually support.

Everybody says they want free enterprise in a democratic market exchange economy that seeks to maximize life engagement, enjoyment, responsibility, and fulfillment. So how come we are currently stuck with the opposite? How could the laziest, least inventive, most crony-connected, monolithic, and parasitic companies siphon up the cash, feast on the bailouts of the industrious, and make it more difficult for us to live a good life? It was not supposed to happen this way, but it did, and it continues to persist.

Part of the problem is that "prosperity" has been degraded and falsified and been made synonymous with getting your "goodies"—profits, entitlements, benefits, windfalls, special favors, and bonuses. Real prosperity created from effort has withered and needs to be revived. We can see with our own eyes that productivity, ingenuity, diversity, and diligence have been either given lip service or taken a good beating in the face of rewarded fraud and self-indulgent consumption. This needs to be inverted.

We can also notice how this latest mutation of capitalism has grown to encompass the global system, since most citizens from Greece to America to China fell for the "too good to be true" hype, including promises of never-ending stratospheric government benefits and forever skyrocketing housing prices and stock valuations.

> *"Don't work for a living. Let your money work for you," became the new mantra. Contributing to society, applying oneself, and caring for others became quaint notions.*

Now that we have tasted the fruits of this false prosperity and experienced the consequent world-wide indigestion, what ought we do?

> *Whatever we do requires a different foundation that rewards and supports productively adding to economies ("making a living") and discourages using the levers of society to parasitically subtract from productive growth ("making a killing")*

Making a living does not need to be eking out survival at an underwhelming job. It can and should mean literally what it says—

"making a life" with all the most energetic and interactive tools at our disposal. Making a killing ought not be the "I've hit the jackpot" bounty that people pretend either. It can and should mean what it literally says— "killing the economy and people's well-being."

Working premises:

- **Free enterprise** means being free to try a new venture, to invest, to save, and to take risks, to protect against risk, to be rewarded financially by the success of your enterprise, and to be rewarded educationally and morally (with learning and character-building) from failures.

- **Applied effort produces value not smoke and mirrors.** Applied effort can include applied manual work, intelligence, creativity, organization, and learning. Applied effort should be aware of its impact and lend something into the world that enables greater capacity. Applied effort can even be things like constructive play that brings fulfillment and enjoyment. Physical health requires applied effort in the form of exercise and dietary discipline. Music and language fluency requires practice. Even "effortless" enlightenment takes great effort. The lives of ostensible masters like Jesus and Buddha were anything but easy. Why should markets be any different?

- **Money does not do work; people do work.** Money, properly understood, is a store of effort (i.e. what pensions are supposed to be) or an exchangeable measure of effort. When money is invested in viable, productive enterprises, it adds the backing of successful effort to a promising enterprise. Thus, one gains a stake in promoting something useful for surviving or thriving and the consequent rewards of growth—not just financial, but also environmental, social, and so forth. Money has no intrinsic worth or merit. It serves and is accountable to other ends.

- **Stakeholdership means "invest the money, effort, and commitment" rather than "take the money and run."** Any healthy enterprise must have people that are fully invested in its success and directly affected by its failures. Playing with other people's money, high-frequency trading, and other examples of exploitation and abuse of honest effort are the opposite of this.

- **Sound public money is the only real money; private fiat currency is purely counterfeit money.** Sound public money is backed by the productive efforts of its citizens. It should be managed on behalf of those citizens and their well-being. Private entities, including the Federal Reserve, who want to create their own private funny money through fractional reserve, leverage, and other forms of fiat backed by nothing are free to do so as a medium of exchange between private parties. However, this private currency should not be redeemed, backed, mixed with, or supported in any way by public money. Leverage is literally "money for nothing" (and from nothing). In addition, leverage, by artificially expanding debt-money, drastically inflates prices of even necessary goods making it very difficult to make a living. (http://market-ticker.org/akcs-www?post=195434)

- **When something seems to be too good to be true, it probably is.** Quick and easy money, when one looks behind that curtain almost always involves deception, exploitation, extortion, or some other abuse or shortcut. This makes easy money damaged goods associated with sweatshops, repressive regimes, environmental pollution, and other practices that strip value and health from our world. This is where our own sense should come in. Twelve percent return on a AAA rated instrument in a bubble economy with record low interest rates? We should know better. It is fake, or it is exploitative.

It is important to note that the current national U.S. economy and global economies do not make any meaningful distinction between healthy and harmful growth. The proliferation of economic cancers embodied in exotic derivatives or housing bubbles are treated as if they were the same as healthy, expanding small businesses that add jobs to a community.

And yes, financial cancer, like biological cancer, does grow very fast as it consumes the economic body, but it destroys that body and should be calculated as a negative in proportion to how much of the productive economy it is destabilizing, dismantling, or replacing.

If the sick care industry is booming due to a dramatic increase in obesity and diabetes in the population, this ought not boost the GDP if one is interested in macro indicators reflecting the health of the economy and its people. You would not treat a cancer patient by considering cancer cells on par with healthy ones, and you should not attempt to heal economies without analogous distinctions.

Part 2: Making a living: Cultivating productivity, ingenuity, diversity, and diligence in a verdant economy

The only "real wealth" here revolves around ability to produce real and needed goods (to allow us to survive), and the ability to create something that increases quality of life (to promote our thriving)." (http://www.oftwominds.com/blogsept11/Zeus-debt-forgiveness-9-11.html)

Free enterprise, well understood and executed,... prizes productivity, quality of life, quality of goods and services, innovation and creativity, transformative learning, honest and diligent labors of love, and enjoyable and engaging relationships and experiences for its citizen members.

These are functions that create health synergistically both for the smaller and the larger, a win-win."
(http://www.oftwominds.com/blogjun10/zeus06-10.html)

> We are coming to the big face-off between top-down control by those who would be gods over us and impose value on us, and bottom up creativity which recognizes that any "god" (energy, good, intelligence) comes up through us and is connected between us. It is this "within" and "between" well-negotiated and exchanged that produces real value." (http://www.oftwominds.com/blogjan11/Zeus-three01-11.html)

Again, "making a living" is "making a life," adding something to an economy, providing a necessary good or service that enhances survival and thriving. In making a living, you are producing something for exchange. You are not merely consuming, nor are you merely taking up space, pushing paper, selling snake oil, or exploiting other people's production. In other words, you cannot make a living by simply being self-serving. You have to provide something of real value to others.

Large corporations and even bureaucracies *can* contribute to making a living, providing everything from swimming pools to social work. Their problems, if anything, center upon what portion of their resources goes into direct service, production, and exchange and how much gets consumed in indirect, personally and institutionally self-serving ends—job justification, bonuses, extravagant salaries, etc. A healthy society maximizes the former and minimizes the latter.

A sane and healthy economy recognizes the need to be "lean and clean," cutting out the fat of self-service and optimizing giving and circulation of pro-social goods and services. This principle is at the root of "value added." This means that corporate welfare in the form of tax breaks for corporations paying their CEOs hundreds of millions of dollars and government workers with gold-plated benefits both need a reality check. They tend to consume more value than they add.

In this, it is time to call out the fallacy of a zero-sum war between personal and social interest. People admit that the most fulfilling personal activities rely upon healthy relationships. Healthy relationships are impossible without giving to others. Our problem stems from failing to practically follow through on our purported convictions:

> What is the economy and society meant to serve? What is most fulfilling and important in life? When asked these questions for themselves and their societies, most people offer answers like: health, family, community, friendship, love, learning, creativity, collaboration, liberty, new experiences, diversity, meaningful work, cultural enjoyment, literacy, curiosity, responsibility, spirituality, faith, and so forth. If you ask those same people how much time, energy, and money they are spending enacting these practices, principles, and values, the answer would likely be (if they were honest), "Comparatively little." (http://www.oftwominds.com/blogjun10/zeus06-10.html)

Aristotle said, "We are what we repeatedly do." He was right. So how might we *do* something different beyond mere talking and imagination? How might we transform economic practices to reflect those activities—giving, production, caring—that we know to be revitalizing. Here are some recommendations meant to provoke possibility:

Investment for the productive long haul: Short term, speculative investing is one of the economy's greatest thorns, distorting stock valuations, bond markets, etc., and destabilizing economies. This is perfectly embodied in the phrase, "play the market." The lion's share of stock market "playing" is not investment or stakeholdership; it is simply gambling and looking for a greater fool to pay more money for a stock.

This mentality incentivizes insider trading, artificially produced volatility, naked short selling (phantom selling to depress value), and a host of other parasitic ventures. Often more profit can be made when a company fails, so there exists an inducement to aid failure, rather than success, in our current unhealthy system.

We certainly could discourage speculation by charging people per transaction for day trades and high frequency trades. However, there are also ways we could reward stalwart investors with a stake in a company's health: Give increasingly greater dividends per share (up to a reasonable point) to people who have stayed with a company longer is one way.

Call it a loyalty premium. This would incentivize sticking through tough times. It would also create a good gauge of stability. If a public record was assembled to display the relative percentages of different types of investors (long-term vs. short term), this could both unmask manipulation and inform potential future investors. If a stock has a high percentage of long-term investors, their satisfaction and return are reflected in their actions, and this provides evidence for a stable investment.

GOVERNMENTS AS SUPPORTERS OF INDIVIDUAL AND COMMUNITY LIFE, NOT SOCIAL ENGINEERS:

Even as a progressive, I support the largely libertarian position on government intervention. For instance, it is not a government's job to subsidize home ownership but to make sure people have a roof over their heads. Keep it simple. Focus only upon those things that promote the core elements of citizens' surviving and thriving.

Surviving: Make the means available to provide for 1) basic food, shelter, and clothing to those who don't have it, 2) medical care for wounds or illnesses, 3) common defense only (not a world-dominating military-industrial complex), 4) environmental protection (so we have clean food, air, and water).

Thriving: 1) Ensure political integrity and proportional representation in voting, legislation, and campaign contributions, 2) uphold both opportunity and ability in developing talent and enforce laws that protect against discrimination on the basis of age, race, sex, sexual orientation, etc., 3) civilly and criminally prosecute financial fraud, counterfeiting, "misreporting," etc., 4) promote pluralistic cultural opportunity, exchange, and practice. Whether it be public prayer, intellectual dissent, or "offensive" forms of freedom of speech, or some other chosen, non-harmful means of expression, government policy should support tolerance and even appreciation of other perspectives.

Local currencies, what Bernard Lietaer in his must-read book, *The Future of Money*, (http://www.lietaer.com/writings/books/the-future-of-money/) calls "complementary currencies" and "work-enabling currencies" apply to community transactions taking place alongside the commercial transactions covered by mainstream economies and monies. Local currencies are "cooperative and sufficient" in operation rather than competitive and scarce, generating additional work and wealth at the local level without causing inflation.

How? Such currencies create a system of formalized exchange of local goods and services in voluntary, rather informal networks that are self-regulated by choice and local supply. This positions local currencies to better and more quickly meet basic needs in a community. They also personalize markets in terms of seeing where one's money goes, keeping wealth circulation local, and better enabling local, small-scale businesses to compete with "big box" stores.

Responsive national monetary policy combined with local currencies creates a workable framework for macro meeting micro and helps ensure that local economies and taxpayers will not be bailing out "too big to fail" banks. As shown in another excellent book, *The Truth in Money Book*, (http://www.truthinmoney.com/main.html), there is a way to design debt-free monetary creation, supply, and management such that it expands and contracts with national economies and populations and challenges the delusions of unending exponential growth.

> A properly balanced money system doesn't do away with borrowing or debt. But it does do away with the impossible demands of an all-debt money system... (A) channel is provided for money to flow into the economy which can be used by people to pay the interests on their debts. This money is debt-free money and when it is extinguished it does not cause a critical money shortage..." (p. 152, *The Truth in Money Book*, 3rd ed., Thoren and Warner).

In this design for the U.S., money is created by the U.S. Treasury and lent to banks, rather than vice versa. The U.S. Treasury has capital requirements guided directly by the needs and size of the national economy. There is no need for fractional reserve, leverage, or original debt.

Independent, non-profit, multi-stakeholder agency setting monetary policy: It is clear that U.S. money creation, supply, and management can neither be handled by Congresspersons beholden to their own careers nor by The Federal Reserve, an agent for private, profit-seeking banks. Politicians have proven they will use fiscal policy to bribe voters by pumping up the welfare state and by cutting special favors for major funders. The Federal Reserve has been a one-stop anti-capitalist shop for bailouts of private banks.

Public interest does not align with either of these constrained purposes. We need an independent body governing monetary policy accountable to the democracy at large, involving the spectrum of stakeholders in proportion to their representation in the populace.

Qualified individuals could be nominated/elected by groups representing various stakeholders. Their qualifications and conflicts of interests could be checked, and they could be appointed to a panel that sets monetary policy. Congress would create money, and this agency would regulate its lending into the economy.

Policy-setting would require deliberation, advocacy, and sacrifices, and hopefully larger citizen education as well. House parties, a la

Howard Dean, could be crucibles for invested, aware citizen discussion of monetary policy trade-offs and options.

Citizen lending and micro lending: We have the technology to skip private banks in the lending process, lend directly from peer to peer, citizen to citizen (http://en.wikipedia.org/wiki/Funding_Circle), and possibly do to banks what Craigslist did to newspaper want ads. We could lend to one another in local currency and national currency and in amounts smaller than would be feasible for profit-seeking banks. Banks and their profit margins and interest rates would have to compete.

Perhaps we could even allow regulated community or non-profit groups to apply for direct lending from the U.S. Treasury at the same rates as private big banks. Again the national interest is upheld by a much more diversified risk, a more stable base of lending, and an economy built on productive real investment and return rather than financialized mumbo-jumbo.

From the national level, money supply could be regulated and inflation managed by interests and taxes in tune with the expansion and contraction for the productive real economy. Strong standards would be established for lending. Lax lending standards by banks would end in borrower default and their own bankruptcy. The value of savings would be magnified as purchasing power would be maintained, and when prices fell due to lower demand, savers could be rewarded for their prudence and foresight.

Savers could buy, invest, and lend and thus expand the economy again creating grass-roots liquidity. When prices for commodities and wages dropped, the national agency regulating monetary policy could work in collaboration with Congress to create money to prudently invest in infrastructure, and thus take advantage of value and spur the job market in a way that makes constituents happier *and* the economy healthier.

"Service swaps" and the end of work as we know it: Jeremy Rifkin and Charles Hugh Smith have spoken extensively about the "end of work" as we know it. There is increasing awareness, due to auto-mation, environmental limits, saturation of the world with material things, open source software and content, etc. (and a growing trend away from possession and toward experience as the arbiter of the good life) that we simply need fewer jobs. Spurring job growth merely for the sake of earning a living, i.e. expanded bureaucracies, is simply no longer sustainable or desirable. We don't have the money to pay for unneeded jobs.

And yet there are multitudes of real needs out there that need to be addressed beyond the purview of mere volunteerism, charity, or government agencies.   There is a huge oversupply of indebted, educated, idealistic young people raring to use their skills and engage their passions. Let's simply have a trade. Make it the business of educational and community groups and institutions to identify, strategize, organize, and meet real needs.

"Hire" people who are unemployed but eager to be active and create a currency exchange where debts, services, and surplus goods can be exchanged (perhaps with local currency) for this pro-social work. Young people, for instance could be hired to care for the elderly, gain from their wisdom and mentoring, and be paid in just-expired food from a grocery store, erased student debt, free movies at community theaters, etc.

This addresses joblessness, waste, and unmet community needs and opportunities in one fell swoop. Supermarkets alone throw out an ungodly amount of perfectly acceptable food, because it exceeds the sell-by date or its apples have a few spots on them. There is every reason to embrace such an obvious opportunity to integrate productivity and waste reduction.

Part 3: Unmaking a killing: Rooting out entitlement, parasitism, fraud, rapacious greed, and other guarantors of destruction

The mission of cancerous economic organizations is to maximize profit, withdraw as much energy as possible, and give as little back as possible. When "maximizing (financial) profit" is allowed to gain power without reference, balance, challenge, or duty, no other cherished capitalist principle can long endure." (http://www.oftwominds.com/blogjun10/zeus06-10.html)

We no longer have a global economic system that is tethered to concrete reality. Parasitic, amoral, slight-of-hand value-shuffling (what I would call the "unreal economy") has effectively trumped the "real economy," the production and exchange of meaningful goods and services." (http://www.oftwominds.com/blogmay10/market-unhinged-from-reality05-10.html)

What constitutes value has migrated from actual value, based in something you earn and related to something you can actually concretely use, to "references to value," some number merely assigned to some financial instrument attached to some good or service somewhere several degrees removed from its source." (http://www.oftwominds.com/blog-may10/market-unhinged-from-reality05-10.html)

We cannot live on bets. We require healthy air, food, water, reasonable housing, and real health care to live." (http://www.oftwominds.com/blogjun10/zeus06-10.html)

Unrest in Greece, rebellion against bank bailouts in Iceland, expanding Occupy Wall Street citizen resistance in the U.S. all signal the coalescing of national grievances into increasingly international movements to bring accountability to the global economy. Right now the injustices are apparent and the basic call to action is plain: "Stop the looting. Start the prosecuting," as summed up nicely Karl Denninger of The Market Ticker. Banks have, to growing public awareness, engaged in multi-tens of trillions of dollars of outright fraud.

Failure to stop the looting and failure to prosecute is quickening the hemorrhaging of world economies, accelerating poverty, depressing asset values, and further creating opportunity for "disaster capitalists" to profit from their own misdeeds and the suffering of others. If this were only about moral hazard, it would be much more manageable.

Instead it is about a system, sanctioned and rewarded at the highest levels of international government, actively abusing and victimizing citizens for greater financial profit. This is full-scale class warfare of the financially powerful *against* free enterprise capitalism and against citizens: "We will take your money, and you will eat our losses, even if we are the ones who created failure."

This Marie Antoinette-style "let them eat cake" arrogance and disconnect has started to make unlikely allies out of working class conservatives and shaggy-haired progressives. This cartoonish ignorance and double-speak by an hyper-entitled class of multi-trillion dollar corporate welfare recipients is only further amplified by images of Wall Streeters pouring champagne on the heads of protesters from balconies and Republican primary contenders fawning over fraudsters and defending Wall Street crimes against accountability.

One hopes citizen voice and action only gain strength under these conditions. The most direct way to clean out rot in the system, of course, is to pursue criminal prosecutions. Those companies and individuals who profited from fraud are receivers of stolen property. Investigate, indict, prosecute, and turn state's witness. Squeeze them. Freeze them— their houses and other assets. Audit their Swiss bank accounts. This would send a strong message that financial violence will be no more acceptable than political terrorism.

However, actual concrete reforms must undergird ousters or criminal convictions. These in turn must reflect productive commitments. Primary among them is the simple notion that people are more important than money. Further, quality of life is more important than profit.

Direct, pure productivity is better than diluted productivity. The fewer intermediaries taking their unwarranted chunk from productive effort the better. If we can all contribute from deeper talent, effort, and aspiration, if we can directly connect with and maintain the sources of a good life minimizing supply chains, commissions, bureaucracies, taxes, and other drains of value, we will all be that much richer.

Now we have to walk our talk and imagine some ways to rehabilitate an entrenched habit of making a killing as a substitute for making a living. Here are some recommendations for getting rid of those parasitic bad habits, money sinkholes, productivity drains, and the twin idiocies of savior state entitlements and corporate welfare:

Promote transparent and accountable markets: Government regulatory agencies were not and are not asleep at the switch; they simply have not been doing their jobs—there is a difference.

During the Bush, Jr. administration, regulatory agencies were staffed by deregulators whose sole purpose was to eliminate safeguards rather than enforce them.

This was done amid a deluded Ayn Randian notion that completely unrestricted markets would regulate themselves and produce maximum benefits for all. The attitude appeared to be: "Everyone can get wealthy by riding the Ponzi scheme of a stock market. Hey let's privatize Social Security too, so old ladies can get in on the action!"

Under the Obama administration, the Department of Justice and regulatory agencies have been essentially instructed to ignore rather than undermine regulations and proper accounting. This was all done under the ironic rubric of "not hurting the little guy" and preventing economic collapse.

Mark-to-market or mark-to-reality accounting rules have been suspended. Not a single major financial player or institution has been investigated even amid hundreds of thousands of proven forged documents in the robo-signing scandals around foreclosures.

Without any federal champion, liberal or conservative, it will fall on voters to insist on citizen-empowered groups at the highest levels to ensure financial rule of law. This is where it would be helpful to have a citizen-accountable board to not simply make recommendations but make actual decisions on pursuing criminal, civil, and bankruptcy proceedings.

In addition it would be a very wise investment to have a public taxpayer team of Elliot Ness-style financial forensics officers like Harry Markopolos (http://en.wikipedia.org/wiki/Harry_Markopolos), who specialize in detecting the double-speak and technical smoke screens in financial reports.

Lastly, citizens must have a publicly funded, publicly accountable board to oversee stock and bond ratings. Moody's, Fitch, Standard and Poor's have proven to be dangerous shills, not ratings agencies. Their collusion makes any trust in their ratings irretrievably compromised.

Get rid of all outright government subsidies and convert them into investments: Government should not be in the business of being Santa Claus. Either a "subsidy" is an investment where the government or other entity gains a stake or it should not be done, period. Seven billion dollar tax subsidies to oil companies like Exxon who was netting at one point 40 billion dollars profit a year is not a break; it is a giveaway.

If taxpayer money is being used to sponsor cutting-edge research that gets monetized by drug companies or technology companies, then the taxpayer (represented by government) should claim patent or intellectual property rights as well as a capital stake in the monetized enterprise. As with venture capitalism, a nice chunk of the profits harvested could be re-invested into other innovations.

We *do* need champions of innovation for big things like energy, medicine, and high-speed internet access and development. The government in collaboration with research universities and non-profits are often the only entities big and broad enough to design and fund these innovations. Innovation, around alternative energy, for instance, is also in the national security interest and could make society healthier, more self-reliant, and more efficient.

But currently government uses taxpayer money to fund research or subsidize a solar company but gets effectively nothing in return. Jobs? Very few jobs come out. Stake in the company? Currently no. If a subsidized company goes bankrupt, the government/taxpayer gets nothing, which is also what they are getting now even when the company is successful.

Incentivize stewardship over "owning": Laws preventing abuse of public-contingent, "private property," and policies encouraging responsible, productive use could be enacted to support in real concrete terms the principle of stewardship. Pay corporate farms not to grow crops? No. Allow them to overproduce using damaging shortcuts like toxic pesticides that poison ground water and cause massive bee die-offs. Also no.

Land should be used responsibly. Why not encourage tax abatements and even job creation and income streams by leasing fertile empty land through an on-line exchange for organic farming, or other healthy, sustainable resource generation purposes. Best practices allowing regenerating land to lie fallow, or to be planted with trees, could also be part of a sane system of maximizing health and productivity for land.

Tax deductions for interest payments on mortgages to support home ownership, on the other hand, are nothing more than a direct subsidy to banks. This privatizing perk should be eliminated. In fact, home ownership should not be the goal; responsible stewardship should be.

> *The current version of "ownership society" does not promote the community stability promised by its advocates. People are renting money from banks hoping to pay off houses with interest payments that often exceed the value of the house.*

Banks bundle up mortgages into impenetrable securities, which are now tanking *and* creating a nightmare of forged titles and transfers. That's not stability. Creating a system where home prices are lower because interest rates are unsubsidized and where peer-to-peer lending is encouraged would insure affordability and recirculation of interest money into the economy.

In addition, market distorting laws like California's Proposition 13 (which artificially suppresses taxes for some and loads tax burdens on others), should be constitutionally overturned as a violation of equal protection, equal treatment, and equal opportunity.

Young couples in a newly purchased "starter" home should never be paying several times more in taxes than million dollar homes bought a long time ago. Nor should corporations be paying pennies on the dollar for their property taxes because they can somehow transfer ownership of commercial properties without actually selling them.

Hit disaster capitalism hard. Have life necessities be stewarded by the public and administered by cooperatives: When one has a healthy respect for humanity, one accepts that no money ought to be made from people's fear or misery. The best way to do this is to have the public take control of necessary resources. Public utilities should in fact be public— controlled and maintained by public cooperatives for public use. Water should not be privatized, but rather conserved and shared by stakeholders in mutual trust, again for the future of the planet and our children.

Whether land or air or water, even food and housing, the necessities of life never were and never are truly owned. They are all produced from resources that are nature's "property," and therefore a gift and nobody's to own. They are also public, and must be managed in the public's interest.

Stewardship in this sense means that you can't do whatever you want with nature's property. You have a primary stewardship obligation to the planet and future generations even if you have a present nominal claim to ownership through a deed or other document.

> *Property deeds do not give you the right to endlessly extract, defile, or otherwise exploit property that was nobody's to begin with and never can be truly owned.*

Encourage giving over receiving: If someone chooses to privately give a gift to a worthy and legitimate charitable organization then, yes, tax advantages should apply because it is a low public cost, productive way to provide support and address need. Again, the working principle involves investing one's self—one's commitment, ones' money, one's support— toward addressing need and aiding opportunity for others and therefore one's self.

Don't guarantee returns for speculative investment or government contracts: It seems heretical, but there should be very little in the way of "guarantee" for returns that are contingent on emerging world and market conditions. "Cost-plus" accounting, no-bid contracts, etc. should simply be disallowed as anti-free enterprise. Guaranteed retirement benefits, 401(k)'s, and even social security payouts have to be responsive to changing conditions in much the same way dividends in companies are reduced or expanded in correspondence with revenue. Even savings are not guaranteed when monetary policy can devastate purchasing power.

Returns have to be pegged to emerging realities and not past promises. If scarcity emerges or can be shown to emerge in the future (i.e. baby boomer bubble), then conservation is called for. Artificial scarcity caused by companies looting pensions or banks flooding economies with fake-asset exotic derivatives, needs to be addressed through prosecution and bankruptcy, where the remaining assets of offending companies are sold off to pay for their scams and the convicted officers of those companies stripped of ill-gotten personal assets and required to do lifetime community service.

Treat Social Security as insurance against poverty, not a bonus or a retirement plan: This almost speaks for itself. When we are concerned with the welfare of others, we realize that certain minimal payments can pull the elderly out of destitution. That was the only historical purpose for Social Security and should remain its purpose. It's not a retirement subsidy. It's there to make sure the elderly, disabled, etc. have sufficient subsistence resources upon which to get up in the morning with a roof over their heads, clothes on their backs and food on their plates. Currently Social Security has become something other. For many, it is their only retirement income. Demands by a growing pool of retirees to support them in a life to which they have grown accustomed would bankrupt younger generations. It would be better to develop housing and community cooperatives with a portion of social security payments so that resources can be multiplied and enjoyment can be increased in old age.

Establish single payer health care, period, primarily administered by local cooperatives: The U.S. pays twice what other countries pay per person for health care and has among the worst actual statistics on important health indicators. Adverse health is one of the leading causes of personal bankruptcy. Small businesses are sagging under the enormous costs of health insurance for employees and thus hire fewer people. American businesses and workers are made less globally competitive because health care costs must be taken out of revenues.

Non-transportable health coverage tied to employment gums up the economy by constraining job mobility and geographic movement. Oh yes, and single payer health insurance would save the U.S. over *400 billion dollars a year,* most of it in reduced overhead (http://www.pnhp.org/facts/single-payer-resources). This could be combined with tough, large-scale, big discount negotiation with drug companies.

These up front savings would be even more enhanced if local cooperatives staffed and supported programs around smoking cessation, weight loss, and nutrition and lifestyle education. If people wanted expensive diagnostics, gold-plated hospital stays, unnecessary plastic surgery, or million dollar interventions to eke out a few more months at end of life then they are welcome to pay for supplementary insurance or use their own cash. Public responsibility for health should involve emphasizing prevention, addressing serious injury and illness, and helping citizens maintain productive, vital lifestyles.

Remove exemptions from anti-trust laws: Be it baseball, health care, big banks, or other, either there is real competition in your arena or you get broken up.

CONCLUSION

About the only guarantee we have in life is one another. We are alternately stuck with or blessed with others. We can make the latter a true resource by developing good will and democratic mechanisms that support a shared productive life.

False "greatness" is also a guarantee—of destruction. Before the catastrophic civil war that erupted in Ancient Greece between Athens and Sparta, the only way to become immortal was to become a war hero. So, what better way to give everyone a chance at immortality then to start endless wars? Well, this mentality essentially wiped out formerly   prosperous   Athens.   (http://en.wikipedia.org/wiki/Peloponnesian_War).

The modern equivalent is probably the material American Dream, where everyone strives for a McMansion and a riding mower. Of course this was always a false dream, dependent upon unsustainable growth and resource use, and eventually simply debt upon debt to maintain. It too has crashed spectacularly.

> *Self-serving dynasties are a very poor substitute*
> *for mutually serving care.*

Dynasties create great injustice and need, and eventually consume themselves. You cannot own the seas or the lands, much less the heavens. You can only own a title, an assignation of a right to live upon or use something. This is really conferrable stewardship. If stewardship has always been the requirement for our fruitful co-existence, and mutually serving care its medium, then we need to open our hearts, spirits, and minds to a very exciting possibility...

We have undiscovered talents to develop and exert. We, who were once distracted, occupied, and oppressed by a glut of consumption, must now use different means to avoid self-destruction and to reach a new frontier. In stepping forward, we take our place in a lineage of generations building something better, higher quality, and more sustainable for our children and the earth upon which we depend to live.

This is never about bombing others into submission, nor about banks creating fictitious financialized wealth so we can be sold on endless riches. Instead, global interest and personal integrity call us to be invested in the social and individual enterprise of a creative, industrious life.

When a false dream is lost, a new and exciting reality is possible.

9
UNLEASHING
THE FUTURE
Advancing Prosperity Through
Debt Forgiveness

How do you administer debt forgiveness? This is not an easy question. "Jubilee" sounds nice, and then you get into the details. Worries about rewarding irresponsible borrowers and punishing responsible and industrious savers inevitably come into the discussion.

Yet we have an even greater problem. Debt is increasing exponentially and the irresponsible and responsible alike are being buried by its excessive demands. From a system level, debt forgiveness will actually help people across the board, because it directly confronts a practical contradiction: Economic growth cannot keep pace with infinite debt on a finite planet.

Material production always plateaus, and it should. Debt does not. So debt will have to be erased in some way. We can choose catastrophic waves of default after a breaking point is reached or we can choose to prepare creative, effective ways to forgive debt in a way that can support future responsibility and spur productivity. This essay is dedicated toward discussing these ways.

INTRODUCTION

My article on debt forgiveness, "Endgame: When Debt is Fraud, Debt Forgiveness is the Last and Only Remedy" (http://www.oftwominds.com/blogsept11/Zeus-debt-forgiveness-9-11.html) must have struck quite a chord in discussions of the future of the economy. It was re-posted on scores of websites and received over 29,000 reads on Zero Hedge. It also resulted in a reference on the Max Keiser Report and a subsequent interview. This led in turn to a popularization of a term I used, "fake assets," to denote the true nature of "toxic assets".

The good news is that people are talking, attempting to assess the situation in real terms, and looking for an alternative to the broken system. The bad news is that this discussion has not been turned very much toward practical directions. The main contention in my original article on debt forgiveness and subsequent interview was simply that ignoring the mathematics of debt (where debt grows exponentially and real growth is limited), especially when magnified by tens, if not hundreds, of trillions of dollars of additional fraudulent debt, is a dangerous fantasy that worsens insolvency and accelerates collapse. "Extend and pretend" cannot provide an answer but can only amplify current destructive trends and delay serious preparation of an alternative.

This article intends to outline some of the alternatives to the current stalemate.

PRINCIPLES AND ISSUES IN DEBT FORGIVENESS ADMINISTRATION:

Before embarking on a mission to address the standoff between people who cannot pay their debts and international economies that have been running on massive debts for the last three decades, one must do a reality check and establish sane observations and principles.

1) **Debt that *cannot* (vs. "will not") be practically paid is not a debt in its classical sense. It's a default.**

   Whether or not people want to recognize this reality is another issue. We recognize that a law that cannot be enforced is not really a law in any practical sense, so why are we dragging our feet with debt? Greece cannot pay its debt by any rational formula. It is already in default. Extending and pretending does not materially change this fact, it only delays recognition of the stark, enduring reality.

2) **Debt based in fraudulent lending is also *not* true debt in any meaningful sense, since the loan along with its obligations originated from something (private fiat) that had no valid authority or exchange value to begin with.**

   Much of the current worldwide debt simply stems from lending based in fraud numbering in the hundreds of trillions of dollars by institutions who did not have adequate collateral (i.e. held insufficient capital reserves, engaged in mark-to-fantasy accounting of their assets, assigned real value to fake assets such as credit default swaps, etc.). A lending body cannot give effectively nothing to someone (claiming it is something) and legitimately expect to get something real back.

3) When debt systems are flooded with fraudulent currencies and claims, it is *not* true that someone, either the borrower or lender, will have to pay the "false value"-backed debt.

You are not legally allowed to profit from crime nor legally obligated to support crime. This precludes the payment of many of the debts currently in circulation. In committing wide-scale control fraud, major financial institutions have broken laws. The laws they have broken are enforce*able*; they just have yet to be enfor*ced*.

However, even with successful prosecution, bankruptcy proceedings, and nationalization/receivership of offending institutions, we are left with a practical problem: Real currency has been mixed with fake currency, real debt with fake debt.

Chains of title and claims to property have been so forged, electronically registered, diced up, and distorted as to make it difficult to sort valid ownership from invalid. When real money has been high-jacked and "disappeared" as with Bernie Madoff, what can be done to address this? These will be points of discussion later in this article.

4) The mathematics of debt, *even without fraud*, would require periodic forgiveness or at least abatement. There must be ways for debts to be adjusted to contingencies.

Economies, like families, go through good and bad times. Debt obligations are constructed as if there are only good times. Basically, the only way to pay off a debt is to outrun it in a time of relative stability. Even in eras of surplus, debt takes a big bite out productive effort, but it quickly becomes consuming as one gets behind in payments and as more and more of the fruits of effort go to servicing debt.

At that point, loans become chains that tie people to mediocre jobs and underwater houses and no longer engines of mobile growth. Debt forgiveness recognizes this contingency and facilitates liberty, productivity, and global quality of life as the more salient indicators of vital economies. Policies and contracts ultimately must be in the interests of people's well-being for them to be legitimate. Conversely, when debt is ring-fenced from contingency, i.e. the exclusion of student loans in bankruptcy, it will be become inherently corrupt as well as unjust.

5) **In any rearrangement of the debt system, productivity and stakeholdership should be rewarded and parasitism should be extinguished.**

It's easy to forget that people used to go to banking agents to get loans to grow their net financial worth through productive enterprise. In such a relationship the bank gained a stake in your success, not your misfortune.

If we are serious about rewarding well-applied effort, then it would make sense to peg debt and debt obligations to the productivity growth curve of an enterprise or domestic product. Lending institutions, then, would essentially buy a longer term stake in the success of enterprises it funds, exert a due diligence proportional to its interest, and both benefit from and share the burden of inevitable rises and falls in growth.

In the housing-bubble debacle the incentives were exactly opposite. Irresponsibility was rewarded precisely because banks could sell off fraudulently documented loans as quickly as they could be signed. In late capitalism, bank support for productivity has been converted into support for exploitation and victimization, using repayment shortfalls to repossess assets from borrowers even though the bank loans were drawn from "money" backed by counterfeit assets.

That has to be reversed—real money for real enterprise backed by real assets.

6) **Things go down and not always up. "New era" rhetoric where financial gravity is suspended is a dangerous delusion.**

When we realize this simple fact and combine it with rewarding productivity and stakeholdership, we realize that our revenues and values will fluctuate dependent upon demand, environmental limits, and a host of other factors, some within our control and some not.

Fighting this empirical fact, on the other hand, creates damaging and unsustainable living. Why not tie notions of prosperity and economic organization to optimizing our productivity, by identifying and working within the changing conditions, not distorting those conditions by taking on debt-credit to be paid by later generations?

7) **The living shall not be beholden to the dead.**

When an individual person dies with debts, what can be collected from their remaining assets is collected and the rest is written off. *Yet the opposite occurs with generational debt. Irresponsible borrowing by past generations is foisted on succeeding generations. The sins of the forefathers are preserved with interest to gouge the quality of life of younger people who neither decided upon nor benefited from irresponsible borrowing.*

Certainly, we now see scorched-earth class warfare of the 1% against everyone else, but we are ignoring an even more profound unintended warfare by an entire generation of post-WWII citizens against the wellness and interests of their own children. How could such a destructive myopia so thoroughly pervade society and bring us this critical historical inflection point? This will be examined in the next part.

FACING FORWARD: EXAMINING GENERATIONAL, HISTORICAL, AND PSYCHOLOGICAL DRIVERS OF DEBT

The demand for credit and debt is driven by generational values, historical habits, and psychological desires. These in turn are premised on evolving notions of the good life. If someone thinks material consumption equates with the good life, then chances are that person will get much farther into debt than another person that values non-material staples as supporting the good life— i.e. family, community, and friendship.

> *Where you put your energy and money communicates strongly the person you are and the way you will interact with the world.*

American baby boomers were born into a world of cheap oil, plentiful jobs, and expansionary foreign policy and were raised by Depression-era parents that wanted to give them the amenities that they never had the chance to enjoy. This engrained an historical sense that physical growth was unlimited and that the "world is there for me".

Today's so-called Millennials (children of baby boomers) are growing up in a starkly different world of peak oil, global warming, shrinking jobs, and diminished material standard of living, but one with unprecedented interconnection. Material opportunities are contracting, but social opportunities are expanding. The new motto emerging is more like: "We are in the world and for each other."

> *Collapsing material prosperity is ceding itself to increasing possibilities for experiential and social richness.*

Consequently, there has been a huge shift in attitudes about the "good life" between generations, largely unnoticed and unreported in traditional media. Only the symptoms of this shift are being reported—social media revolutions, Arab Spring, the Occupy Wall Street movement, young popular dissident authors in China (http://www.nytimes.com/2011/11/07/world/asia/murong-xuecun-pushes-censorship-limits-in-china.html), and pop-driven musical critique of conservative fundamentalism in Pakistan (http://www.nytimes.com/2011/11/07/world/asia/beygairat-brigades-youtube-hit-song-challenges-extremism-in-pakistan.html).

The motivating underlying philosophy for younger generations, has not been effectively brought to light. Around the world there has been a coalescing of youth around active principles of liberation, opportunity, and creativity energized through fulfilling *experience and application* as the currency of the good life. This stands in contrast to older generations where *possession* was the ideological linchpin of the good life, driven by desires for security, entitlements, and predictability.

This has enormous implications for the world economy and each generation's relationship with debt. Younger generations don't want to own things as much as they want to be able to access them and use them (think "shareware"). As a result non-material goods (relationships) or quasi-material goods (access to the internet) are gaining greater importance than material goods (huge LCD TVs).

According to the prevalent thinking of many young people, useful debt leverages utility around experience and development, more than the acquisition of material goods. Credit should be used as an investment to expand experiential personal and interpersonal growth opportunities that pay different kinds of dividends, whether a job (money to do other things), education (learning), travel (diversity), a peak experience (enjoyment), or funded time as a volunteer (service). The focus is on the "use" not on the "thing".

"USE VALUE" VS. "THING VALUE"

Sharing resources and goods is more attractive to younger generations because it reinforces experience and relationship. Consumption for consumption's sake is at odds with this preference. Again most consumer credit has been extended to buy unnecessary things, even as these unnecessary things have driven a global consumer economy. This along with government entitlement programs and military spending has been largely responsible for U.S. consumer debt and national debt.

Younger generations are simply not willing to buy into entitlement and consumption at anywhere close to the same scale as their parents. They rightfully see these pyramid schemes as rigged: as generationally unfair (i.e. federal entitlements), environmentally untenable (heavily wasteful of energy and material), and undesirable from a lifestyle standpoint (requiring more money and additional time and energy to purchase and maintain then they are worth) (http://welearnsomething.blogspot.com/2011/05/tedx-tokyo-let-junko-edahiro-welcome.html).

This "use value" focus of youth is in many fundamental ways incompatible with "thing value" assumptions of previous generations.

Even if they wanted to go the way of their parents, Millennials know they can't. The world won't support it. This massive decrease in consumption by the young will ensure a steep drop in the need for debt but require a radical creativity in world economic premises and organization.

The post-WWII mindset, "I need to get mine, so asset values have to go up and up," warped credit supply and assessments of reality, especially in the housing market. Driven by historical patterns and psychological desires, it became an article of faith that house prices could only go up, not only "up" but "very up" so everyone can get rich! This mode of thinking and acting naturally led to the housing bubble.

Without easy credit the nominal market value of houses, what people are willing or capable of paying for, has dropped rather precipitously. This price retracing reflects not losses but erasure of false value, readjustments of nominal value to reality.

This dynamic between "use" and "thing" value plays itself out even in ideas of social progress. Those inclined toward possession-oriented, "thing" value, feel and act on an underlying assumption that the more money and attention they can attract to themselves, their cause, or their organization the better the world will be.

People of this mindset end up counterproductively vying against each other to be the lead spokesperson in "saving the world," thus fracturing limited resources in order to fund limited visions in a situation that fundamentally requires cooperation to be effectively solved. To be viable, personality and mission-driven idealism will have to cede itself to collaborative problem-solving pragmatism, i.e. "use" over "thing."

> *"It's mine," only makes sense if you deny your own mortality.*

Rather, you have responsibility for something in your temporary care and control. In fact the burdens of ownership—insurance, maintenance, storage, time, taxes—are seen by many in the younger generation as getting in the way of the good life. Nominal ownership is preferred only insomuch as it may create opportunity for autonomy (i.e. doing what you like to your house without interference from a landlord).

> *There is a new mandate emerging: It's about what you can do for others as a facilitator of life growth, not solely what you can do for yourself, the self-consumed mover and shaker, the approval-needy individual.*

Much of the past psychology of debt and the failed material American Dream, involves people "taking and expanding"—taking on any debt liability and using what ever credit means necessary to build a heroic narrative: "My big house, my great reputation, my huge salary all must grow (exponentially) to Olympian heights."

This mentality is based in things that one "owns." Even non-material qualities like identity, ideology, reputation, celebrity, and character have been commodified and bought and sold in this framework. Eliminate this need to seek self-affirmation through consumption and commodification, and you can immediately eliminate many trillions of dollars of potential debt.

Status-oriented worth also leads to a desire to cut corners, to engage in fraud to aggrandize one's image. When you distort the image around a "thing," whether that thing is one's reputation or a "complex" exotic financial derivative, it is a lot easier to misrepresent value and to dupe others.

When a thing has to prove its value in actual use, then it becomes a lot more difficult to misrepresent its worth. Bernie Madoff extracted his illegal profits through his reputation. People did not closely examine his actual investment products. People focused on "who he was" and not "what he did." The first refers to "thing value"; the second has to do with "use value" and quality.

> *A society based in individual heroism, guarantee, and*
> *security will in all likelihood destroy itself.*

Why? If your own narrative, wealth, power, and image in the eyes of others is paramount, you won't risk your status in learning, making mistakes, or trying new approaches when the old approaches fail. If you merely look at your own situation, and use your negotiating power to leverage greater benefits from larger arenas, you tend to become isolated from the needs of others. You become entitled, believing that others create their own fate and that you alone "earned your benefits."

Entitled individualism also erodes the skills and perspectives needed to analyze challenges on a systemic scale and cooperate with others in order to meet those challenges. "Thing value" and the habits that go with it are not only obsolete but quite hazardous in the present context. *They also cost too much.* Politicians can promise gold-plated benefits to everyone, but they won't be able to deliver. They are hoping you vote based on a promise, not its viability. The cure: Vote on reality, not wish.

Today's youth care relatively little about your reputation, your estimate of yourself, or your pretty speeches. They want to know, "What exciting phenomenon can you produce or create?" "What inspiring ideas or provocative words can you contribute to this larger conversation?" "What actions have you taken to solve the problem?"

This goes for young people in deciding about the performance of politicians. They will not simply pledge their allegiance to a politician based on hype or past support. They ask instead, "Have you exerted your power on behalf of opportunity for all? Have you stayed connected to us? Have you ensured fairness? Have you gotten the job done?" For Obama the answer has come back a stout, "no," so the younger American generation has little use for him except as a placeholder against a worse candidate.

The same is true for the promises of great prosperity if young people just take out stratospheric student loans to pay off their overblown university education costs. That promise is not panning out (http://www.ibabuzz.com/education/2010/10/07/close-the-achievement-gap-graduate-college-then-what/). A new way forward is required and young people know their lives depend upon it.

Older generations have a choice, to extend and pretend and hope they die before the consequences show up, or change premises and learn to serve a larger purpose in tune with the younger generations. This will be discussed in the next parts.

ADMINISTERING DEBT FORGIVENESS TO RESTART THE GLOBAL VALUE SCALE, PROMOTE PRODUCTIVITY, AND ENSURE FAIRNESS

Ultimately, debt forgiveness starts from the need for global social self-preservation. Succeeding generations will not or cannot continue the easy credit charade, so zeroing out debt, prosecuting fraud, and pursuing bankruptcies to those who have overextended themselves, including "too big to fail banks," is necessary to get the monkey off the back of the global economy and future generations. However, this will have to be done so as to prevent future abuse, open up opportunity, and reinforce a healthy productivity.

Again, when debt is both unsustainable and largely fraud, debt forgiveness is the last and only remedy. No other responses have come close to adequately dealing with the systemic enormity of the problem. Current conventional attempts at reform are some version of "extend and pretend" ("solving" debt with more debt) or "hide and seek" (valuating assets mark-to-fantasy and stashing liabilities off the books). Those are not solutions; they are pipe dreams.

Productivity, prosperity, and well-orchestrated debt forgiveness align on one side, and austerity and debt expansion align on the other side in this challenge. We've already seen the trajectory of the latter choice. It accelerates concentrations of wealth and control, damaging democratic governance, creating personal misery (as seen with upticks in those in poverty and without medical care), stirring violence and unrest, and destabilizing societies.

*When the wrong things are being valued and rewarded,
people have the right and duty to resist,
and they **are** resisting.*

Currently present and future generations are literally and metaphorically being imprisoned through the attempted enforcement of non-enforceable and fraudulent debt.

How is paying off a hopeless mortgage any different than house arrest?

In this climate, debt forgiveness is based on a very clear and rational decision: Restorative justice for people currently paying off fraudulent or untenable liabilities (largely run up and foisted on them by others) is more important than worrying about selected opportunists "taking advantage of the system" to escape valid debts.

In other words, the system is far more broken than the people in it.

If transformed with canny foresight and wisdom, a renewed system can actually reward those willing to produce and insist upon other forms of pro-social volunteer effort as "payment" for those who do not have money. This is called picking up the pieces and working in good faith.

ARGUMENTS FOR AND AGAINST DEBT FORGIVENESS: FACTS AND FALSEHOODS

When confronted with the option of debt forgiveness, many citizens argue that loans are some kind of sacred cow and that debt forgiveness would reward irresponsibility. Their simplistic truisms usually ignore context and inevitably focus on the moral or contractual obligations of low-level operators and borrowers ("You signed it; you have to pay it off no matter what.").

The context and truth is this: Massive debts have been run up in our global financial system at all levels. The most egregious debts have been incurred by those with the most power and by those enriching themselves by extracting financial flesh from taxpayers and borrowers.

So let's get dispense some truth and confront the myths:

The biggest thieves, the most immoral, criminal, and irresponsible debt players by far have been those who have been enriched the most from our current debt system. Mom and pop underwater mortgage holders are not the problem.

Look no further than "too big to fail banks" who profited enormously from fraud in the lead-up to financial meltdown, blew up the system in 2008, got bailed out with tax payer money, and then promptly rewarded themselves with a record 144 billion dollars in compensation a year later.

Unexpected events can wipe out even responsible savers and well-administered finances.

Even if a borrower takes out a loan that he or she can comfortably afford and saves up a six-month emergency fund, that borrower can get behind through illness or job loss or other unanticipated event. For larger borrowing economies these events could be peak oil or global warming or any number of strains that are not accounted for and that significantly interrupt or alter growth trajectories.

Add to this modern finance where money-to-debt ratio is widening through fractional reserve banking and complex leveraging, and we can note that *only a small fraction of total debt could physically be paid off.* That means morally–and practically–objectionable debt slavery for the vast majority of loan holders, as their productive efforts go into paying off interest to faceless institutions rather than investing in families and communities.

As mentioned earlier:

1)   Debt that *cannot* be paid is already default. By this measure many countries (Greece, Italy, Spain, U.S.) are already in default. Pretending otherwise, through austerity and similar measures, will simply stress the body politic to the breaking point and beyond.

2)   Current debt is unenforceable because people do not have the money, jobs, or assets to pay them due to unprecedented global economic contraction.

3)   There is so much fraud and counterfeit value in the current system (700 – 1,000+ trillion in the derivatives market alone), that current real assets cannot cover liabilities.

4)   Government welfare promises/entitlements in most countries, due to a post-WWII population bubble, far outstrip the capacity of future generations to deliver on them.

> By laboring under a "debt as natural/moral law" delusion, world economies are trying to essentially drain the sea of international debt by bailing the sea into the boats of national economies and on to the backs of productive citizens.

This approach is not working; that sea of international debt is growing beyond control due to its colossal size coupled with compound interest.

We know that national austerity cannot come close to solving this predicament, so why are we pretending? The truth is that regular citizens are not pretending. They have to live the reality of increasing debt and diminished material opportunity. It is powerful leaders and the financial honchos who have covered their eyes and distanced themselves from the consequences of their own collapsed designs.

This peek-a-boo approach of current world leaders will only delay the day of reckoning and thus make the economic and political consequences worse. This blithe irrationality and cowardice is a recipe for violent revolt, economic freeze-up, panic, shortages of vital goods, and, ironically, endangerment of those leaders themselves.

Ordered deleveraging will not be sufficient at this point, since levered value has already illegally been converted into counterfeit value by an unregulated shadow banking system. This counterfeit "notional" value not only swamps people's ability to pay, but might even eclipse the value of real assets (unless, of course, you mark those to fantasy as well).

Even an egomaniacal two-year-old will grudgingly admit that there are no more cookies in the jar once he as eaten them all. This is far better than adult bankers who decided to make up imaginary "cookies" to dispense from that same jar (based on leverage or fractional reserve), and then expect people to hand them back real cookies (money, labor, and assets) in exchange for these concocted cookies.

When we support debt forgiveness we are left with a zeroed scale, and therefore any "cookie" added will be from our own creativity, effort, and good sense. That is a far better place to proceed from than less-than-zero where our efforts go to resupply imaginary value.

*The system is **not unsustainable;** it is already **broken.***

The system needs to be put on a path of real, concrete productivity and growth (labor, learning, creative application, quality of life, etc.), not malignant expansion of credit and debt. My argument is that debt forgiveness is an essential mover in this necessary transformation. It is best for debt in its current ideological form, to be decisively repudiated in practice and replaced with a working system based on healthy, productive principles.

This process of debt repudiation and financial transformation includes extinguishing delusional, segmented economic practices that promote leeching from the future and "internalizing gains and externalizing liabilities." Instead we recognize and act within an inherently interconnected system where we "pay forward" our talents and investment in the growth of a stronger, safer, and more solvent future.

This will be discussed in the next part.

PAYING FORWARD: PRODUCTIVITY PRINCIPLES AND COMMITMENTS

Simply put, "productivity" is giving to the future, instead of taking from the future. Parasitism is the opposite: Borrowing from the future to fund present desires without credible connection to future healthy growth. Successful productivity requires the development of beneficial new approaches to value creation and the rigorous identification and confrontation of approaches that destroy value and that destroy the environmental, financial, social, and personal fabric of human endeavor.

> *Debt forgiveness is initially brought into play to erase a consuming burden, but cannot be viable over the long haul without affirmative new ways to create and exchange value.*

Given that we have the collective integrity, self-preservation instinct, human will, and the sense of necessity to confront our broken system, let's first establish philosophical and practical principles to guide debt forgiveness as "giving to the future instead of taking from it":

1) Vitality and worth of debt forgiveness decisions and policies will be assessed on the opportunities they create broadly and systemically, not simply confine themselves to individual cases.

2) Debt forgiveness will support global health and significantly exceed "sustainable," including creating surplus productivity and opportunity for future generations and not just mitigating current practices.

3) Debt forgiveness and subsequent laws will ensure future legal lending is tied to productivity rather than parasitism, in other words, to the success rather than failure of the borrower.

4) Debt forgiveness will acknowledge that private failures and liabilities will be handled by the private parties involved and not simply offloaded to government.

5) Debt forgiveness will promote autonomy and sovereignty not dependence.

6) Debt forgiveness will develop, utilize, and support the metric of actual "use value" over arbitrary mark-to-model "thing value."

7) Debt forgiveness will have the requirement of breaking up monopolies standing in the way of a true discovery of "use value."

CASE APPLICATIONS OF DEBT FORGIVENESS THAT CONFRONT PARASITISM AND REWARD PRODUCTIVITY

With the Occupy Wall Street (OWS) movement, people are beginning to turn their attention toward fully engaging society's corrupted and powerful decision-makers and creating their own productive alternatives. Changing a system demands something greater from a citizen than merely voting. It means coordinated action on behalf of the public interest.

The success of 650,000 people "moving their money" (4.5 billion dollars) from "too big to fail" banks to local banks and credit unions offers a template of what coordinated effective citizen resistance and proactive alternatives might involve (http://www.washingtonsblog.com/2011/11/big-banks-plead-with-customers-not-to-move-their-money.html).

How can we effectively administer debt forgiveness that breaks our habit of stealing from the future *and* creates surplus in health and social wellness? The following examples will briefly analyze current primary debt arenas and dynamics, propose debt forgiveness strategies to confront parasitism (along with citizen strategies to break up monopolies responsible for most of the parasitism), and suggest viable alternatives going from the smallest to largest debt arenas— personal (credit cards), family (mortgages), generational (student loans), national (deficit spending), and global (environmental damage).

CREDIT CARDS: THE PERSONAL IS ECONOMIC

Analysis: In 2008, consumer credit debt in America was about 0.85 trillion dollars. Two companies, MasterCard and Visa have a virtual monopoly on the processing end of consumer credit (with American Express and Discover rounding out the quartet) (http://www.nerdwallet.com/blog/credit-card-data/average-credit-card-debt-household/)

Credit card companies are multi-tens of billions of dollar businesses processing trillions in transactions that claim centrality to commerce because they ostensibly reduce transaction time and add ease, convenience, and record-keeping. However, they often are hugely parasitic, charging 3+% to businesses for using their service, 35.00 dollars for late fees, 30+% interest after missing a payment, and the list of excesses goes on.

With advancing technology, consumer charging and credit is becoming a relatively simple matter. It certainly would be possible to re-place especially the debit function, break up the monopolies, and keep the convenience (http://articles.businessinsider.com/2011-11-11/tech/30381380_1_credit-card-interchange-fees-paypal).

Too many people are dependent upon consumer credit to pay for necessities like food, rent, medical care, and even education, so that must be addressed in debt forgiveness around consumer credit.

Intervention: Allow for (and protect/promote the right of) people to file for bankruptcy and discharge their credit card debt completely. If credit companies played fast and loose with on-paper profits and stepped up interest rates, then they should experience the consequences of overreach, i.e. default. Next time they should do a better job at ensuring collateral, looking at income, and being judicious with credit lines. The consequence for the consumer is a bad credit rating and the possibility of being refused future credit.

Credit companies can strike a deal to settle part of the debt in exchange for a preserved credit rating. That is already done now. The point is to wean people from unnecessary credit. To address those who rely on revolving credit to meet basic life needs, communities can help by creating local currency-based surplus supply and exchange networks for housing, food, certain medical care, and other necessities (http://www.oftwominds.com/blogoct11/making-a-living-Zeus-pt2.html).

Going forward, it may simply be beneficial to cut out transnational corporations altogether, and once again re-awaken the tradition of local tabs for goods and services. For online purchases, there is an increasing array of charging options, and more could be developed by savvy citizens, non-profits, and start-ups.

MORTGAGES: INDENTURED FAMILIES

Analysis: According to U.S. census data, mortgage debt totaled 13.8 trillion dollars at the end of 2010, 9.3% of which was delinquent (or about 1.3 trillion) (http://www.census.gov/compendia/statab/cats/banking_finance_insurance/payment_systems_consumer_credit_mortgage_debt.html). With money like that in play and almost zero regulation, it is no wonder that housing was ripe for extreme manipulation. Between skyrocketing prices driven by easy credit, appraisal fees, tax revenue gains, transfer fees, etc., there was a lot of incentive to let the crooked times roll.

Now we have a full-blown extended housing bust with banks hiding the true nature and value of their mortgage loan "assets" turned liabilities. Homeowners are being caught in a no-man's land of not being able to renegotiate reasonable principal reductions or tenably refinance, and taxpayers are being asked to backstop the housing debacle through government agencies like Fannie Mae and Freddie Mac to the tune of hundreds of billions of dollars.

House sales are depressed. Nothing's moving. People are holding their collective breath. Many predict and fear hysterical overshoots in housing prices to the downside. Government policies seem intent on trying to re-inflate housing prices.

Intervention: It doesn't seem prudent to simply encourage everyone who cannot pay their current mortgage to default and thus force the mass selling of mortgage-related assets just to get at the "true value" of unsold and defaulted inventory. Prices probably would crater. Panic likely would ensue, leading to a disordered cascade of insolvencies. However, we cannot stay where we are and tread water for a couple of decades nor can we re-inflate the housing bubble. A kind of "middle path" debt forgiveness might be the reasonable course here.

Why not simply establish as part of debt forgiveness a coordinated common metric that housing be pegged to the inflation index for affected regional markets. Housing has followed that inflation index almost to a tee in the last 100 years. This is another way of saying that houses and land do not, in fact, gain relative value, but merely increase in price to keep even with dollar purchasing power. Land and houses in this scenario become a maintenance store of value, then, and not a phony producer of increased value.

Peg the loan interest rates for underwater homeowners to the bank savings rates (which are now almost zero), and add in only reasonable loan servicing costs. The point here is to break even, and move inventory in such a way that neither advantages nor disadvantages parties. If banks become insolvent in this arrangement, then they need to be taken into receivership and processed by the appropriate regulatory agencies.

Homeowners who cannot pay in the new value scale will default and move out. Others will have lower payments, but their homes will be worth nominally less asset-wise. These latter homeowners will have already suffered a hit and learned a lesson about living within their means in the inflated payments and interests they've already made. Houses that took advantage of this program would be price and time percent limited on subsequent ownership transfers and rental rates to prevent abuse and to allow more diverse populations to vie for housing in particular areas.

If one then eliminates government tax subsidies associated with mortgage interest, and proposes only fees associated with maintaining and servicing homes (municipal taxes, loan administration overhead, etc.), you have a fairly reasonable approximation of value, a "growth" in price which primarily maintains the purchasing power of the dollar, but adds no phony or subsidized "wealth".

A house becomes something to live in. Nothing added. Nothing taken away. This is consistent with the principle that, in the interest of quality of life, necessities like basic food, housing, clothing, water, and medical care should not be treated as cash cows.

Moving forward as citizens, instead of focusing on the nominal asset value in home ownership, there is an opportunity here to focus on use-value: "How much does this or that obligation or opportunity support my larger, deeper physical, financial, mental, and spiritual health?"

> *If the nominal price of a house is too high to keep one out of debt slavery and directly serve deeper purposes, then either refuse to buy it, sell it, or default on it. Its use value is negative.*

Instead, share a house, invest in a housing cooperative, or rent a house within your means. Even a house that has lost "thing" value (asset value), has largely maintained its "use value". By focusing on use value we can combat the human penchant to psychologically obsess over the roller coaster of nominal asset gains and losses.

Sales commissions, especially large ones, invite skewed risk evaluation, conflict of interest, and price inflation. For this reasons reputable sources will always advise potential customers to get a flat-fee or hourly rate professional for financial planning.

However, the same logic holds true for realtors and mortgage brokers. To break up those monopolies, citizens could team up to insist on flat-rate assisted selling/buying and to create Wiki-like databases making house purchase information fully transparent and available (in a way that goes beyond MLS listings and National Association of Realtor propaganda).

In addition circle and peer-to-peer lending could be developed further with technology along with updated practices to create a pathway around banks and brokers in financing a home. These moves could significantly increase housing market volume and mobility by decreasing transaction costs and eliminating dependence on middlemen.

STUDENT LOANS: GENERATIONAL CON GAMES

Analysis: Total university student loan debt has passed the one trillion dollar mark in the United States, 100+ billion of that in 2010 alone (http://www.usatoday.com/money/perfi/college/story/2011-10-19/student-loan-debt/50818676/1). College tuition has risen 7.45 %/year in compounded terms since 1978, doubling the inflation rate and far outpacing even the outrageous increases in health care costs. (http://mjperry.blogspot.com/2011/07/higher-education-bubble-college-tuition.html).

It seems astounding that something, higher education, so intrinsic to personal growth, economic well-being, and the viable future of the world has been held hostage by a monopoly consortium of public and private "higher" education institutions charging such exorbitant and unjustified prices.

No one seems to be advocating for the student. On the contrary, there is an incentive for turnover and student failure. Predatory private lenders gain greater profits through collector's fees and penalties if students default. They can then send the hollowed-out remainder off to the government guarantor.

For-profit colleges like Phoenix University get to keep semester tuition payments even if a student drops out after four weeks. These private agents don't care how inflated their promises were. They have the students' money. Legislators don't seem to seriously care either, since they can use taxpayer money to backstop student loan default after they promise better deals to young voters.

Today's college students graduate with record debt and enter a world of unprecedented economic contraction. The promised high-paid jobs are not there. Even many of the fairly low-paying entry-level jobs are scarce. An entire generation of aspiring youth is being set up for life-time debt slavery unless some form of debt forgiveness can be worked out.

President Obama's recent "Pay as You Earn" plan to re-gauge repayment of student debt seems to have some valid ideas like basing loan repayment on a percent of income (10%) and limiting student debt horizon to a maximum number of years. However it only covers debt incurred since 2008 for people who have not yet graduated college (http://bostinnovation.com/2011/10/31/what-president-obamas-student-loan-forgiveness-plan-means-for-you/).

It thus excludes a vast majority of young debtors and nearly all of the current trillion dollars of student loan debt. That is not forgiveness; it's vote-appeal rhetoric that does not actually challenge the parasitic players.

Intervention: Is there an alternative in the near term? Is there an option besides civil resistance and unilateral intentional default (http://www.thenation.com/article/164686/students-debt-cant-pay-wont-pay-dont-pay)? Effective debt forgiveness and applicable policy have to bring everyone in as stakeholders in the post-graduate success of college students and, thus, the larger society that depends upon productive citizens.

> *Debt payments have to be aligned with economic productivity curves and economic contingencies instead of simply extracting more from the borrower regardless of context.*

This means due diligence, support, and re-negotiation if necessary. Private loans should not be government guaranteed, and they should exert the same lending standards as those required for small business loans. Government loans, especially for financially riskier or disadvantaged students, might accept non-financial productivity currency as debt payment (i.e. pro-social work as a national volunteer).

Colleges who dramatically underperform on their promises and to industry standards should be required to refund a portion of the tuition they received, the same as any business would with defective merchandise. In principle, each student should be granted the opportunity to pay off student loans as a percentage of income ending in complete forgiveness after a fixed term (pro-rated to total debt) or erase student debt altogether in exchange for specified pro-social volunteer work.

> *Why not preclude university debt in the first place by creating competitive alternatives to the current monopolies of high-priced school lending and low-delivery higher education?*

Why not have community sponsorship for students who commit to coming back and sharing their skills, as we sometimes see for rural doctors?

Why not take advantage of circle and peer lending to borrow from pools of citizen-invested capital and cut out parasitic private lending? Why not develop and accredit alternative education which focuses on practical application of knowledge?

Why not make professional certification a customized process of achieving certain high standards on publically available tests, internships, and practicums? Wouldn't this reward outcomes and spur innovation, time-saving, and accessible learning?

DEFICIT SPENDING: NATIONAL ABSURDITY, INTERNATIONAL GAMESMANSHIP, AND MANIPULATION BY TRANSNATIONAL CORPORATIONS

Analysis:

> *If you look closely and truthfully, the major global economies, the U.S., China, the European Union, et. al., are collectively insolvent and engaging in massive interactive fraud, mutual exploitation, and misrepresentation of national financial health.*

The U.S. as the overseer of reserve currency is trying to print its way back into solvency and its banks, like Goldman Sachs, have provided the poison pills for EU implosion with their fraudulent derivatives.

Europe will not face the facts that it has unsustainable welfare state commitments and that its banks extended credit and covered debt for Greece, Italy, Portugal, Spain, and Ireland (often through private banks in those countries) that were not warranted and could not be paid back.

China (the current growth darling) is devaluing its currency, destroying its environment, poisoning its population, experiencing growing unrest, separation of wealth, collapse in real estate values, and corruption in governance in the government's effort to maintain unsustainable growth, trade imbalances, and grip on autocratic power.

> *The real threat, however, to the global economies is not nation against nation but transnational corporations allied with so-called "ruling elites" against the vast majority of the world's population.*

This alliance is intentionally playing nations against each other in an effort to control, maximize, and concentrate parasitic wealth in the hands of a global few at the expense of productive citizens.

There has been no better evidence of this than the eerie world-wide cover-up and bailing out of derivatives and bank fraud, the non-prosecution of hundreds of thousands of confirmed cases of forgery over private property conveyance (United States), the Libor scandal, rehypothecation and derivatives fraud (England), the hollowing out of national revenue and well-being through austerity (Ireland), and the stripping of national assets and sovereignty (Greece with more to come).

"Bought and sold" has acquired a whole new level of meaning.

Intervention: Growing awareness and unrest are beginning to challenge this pattern, but what are its implications for debt forgiveness? Hopefully global movements will lead to much needed turnover in world governance or non-violent social revolution and civil disobedience that renders illegitimate the hold current government leaders have on power.

Frog marching bank executives and other abusers of the global public trust in front of the International Criminal Court could bring the same legal and moral accountability that applies to ruthless dictators. These abusers could be charged, convicted, and thrown in jail, their personal assets confiscated, and their Swiss banks accounts raided, or (if one is to get into the spirit of forgiveness) they could be required to do community and national service for the rest of their lives to compensate for the damage they have caused.

> *Nations who finally elect people of integrity in government with the wisdom to recognize imminent environmental, cultural, social, political, and economic interdependence and the fortitude to prosecute international financial criminals would be well advised to collectively zero out national debts.*

What countries owe one another is a pittance compared to aiding and abetting of hundreds of trillions of dollars of publicly supported private fraud. Even "real number" debts have dubious foundations: The U.S. supposedly "owes" China a trillion dollars or so, but China has likely taken at least that amount from the U.S. in intellectual property theft (industrial patents, computer software, and entertainment) as well as the sale of counterfeit brand name goods.

The same unregistered reciprocity exists with the couple of trillion or so the U.S. owes India and Saudi Arabia. India has benefited massively from the public U.S. university system and the private offshoring of technology jobs, and Saudi Arabia has been able to hold a stable grip on its repressive power largely with the implicit backing of U.S. foreign policy and military muscle.

What might emerge after international debt forgiveness in a more interconnected and cooperative world? Perhaps a global currency will come into existence, based on a kind of "Esperanto dollars," backed by some agreed upon standard of exchange value.

> *I would not be surprised to see formal national money take a backseat to voluntary forms of exchange and trade like local currencies or swapping of services, skills, and information.*

Environmental damage: Global pollution and resource abuse as debt

Analysis:

> *We ought to treat as massive debt the kind of "borrowing"*
> *we have taken from Mother Nature in the form of resource*
> *extraction and deposit of "toxic liabilities" in the form*
> *of pollution. This debt is physical It cannot simply be*
> *erased. It has to be paid back in the form*
> *of wise use and environmental healing.*

This debt will not be forgiven by more trickery or a fundamentalist belief in the magic of the market, though creative market responses will be essential to slowing damage and creating sustainable opportunities.

I am highly suspicious of speculative markets like carbon trading, just as I am of speculation in water supply. These arenas are too intrinsic to human survival to be toyed with in largely abstract, remote, and ripe-for-abuse speculative market posturing.

Debt forgiveness here really involves a whole-scale transformation about how we relate to ourselves, to each other, and to the world around us. Honoring our debt to nature means that we recognize our pursuit of happiness depends upon our physical sustenance.

Intervention: This will require comprehensive education, re-grounding in natural experience, and recommitment to simple living to pay down the massive debt of ignorant living to which we have grown accustomed.

It will call for an evolution of ideas of the good life that move from physical manufacturing, use, and exploitation of the material world, to one where the material world provides only the bare support needed to explore, expand, and develop our increasingly non-material opportunities and aspirations.

I personally find this a heartening and exciting direction, but many are likely to view it as a step down. This will be one of the most important global conversations in the next century.

Conclusion:

> *Financial debt is not a natural phenomenon or a moral law. It is created by humans and can be erased by humans.*

There is nothing moral about a nation running up its children's national credit card to the tune of 14 trillion dollars (with another 100 trillion+ in federal entitlements) and expecting the next generation to pay for it. Nor is it morally reasonable to expect individual people, who have worked hard and followed the economic rules, to suffer with life-long debt servitude for mid-game changes in the rules and shifts in the global context.

In point of fact, our current "sea" of international debt is merely a very large man-made lake, damned up by ignorance, greed, and exploitation. The only healthy way to manage current debt is to drain this lake completely through debt forgiveness.

> *It is time to take down the debt dam and let democratic prosperity flow.*

True, people will not get their individual material dreams and hopes of unlimited riches fulfilled, but they will take important steps toward preventing a war of humanity against humanity, and they will be able to engage new opportunities and definitions of the good life involving working together creatively to build a better, more just world.

> *Instead of propping up an old dream where we impose*
> *past fantasies on a dynamic future, we can embrace a*
> *new dream— creating, exploring, expressing, unfolding,*
> *and reinventing who we are through shared, interactive*
> *improvement and accomplishment.*

The old economic system based on scarcity and false security is thus converted toward new ends—freedom, health, quality of life, creativity, autonomy, and mutuality. In pursuing this progress in jubilee, we advance a long way toward clearing out our past entrapments, inequities, and animosities.

We then wisely devote our shrinking material resources toward developing experiential, non-material, and social exchange that multiplies abundance and increases in value the more it is shared.

10

'I GIVE A DAMN'

*A Capitalist Manifesto for the
Productive Class*

The title speaks for itself. This essay is a call to citizens to put real work, ingenuity, and community above false promises and disgraced authority. Empowerment, in this essay, is not about pumping up self-esteem but rather equipping citizens to take control of the global economy. When political and economic leaders fail to act effectively, we will have to be the ones to succeed.

> *Capitalism stands and falls upon care, not the superficial "I-feel-your-pain" type, but the deep, committed "I-give-a-damn" type.*

WHAT DOES IT MEAN TO GIVE A DAMN?

"I give a damn" means: I get broadly and deeply involved, I refuse to ignore what is going on around me, and I confront and respond to challenge. The operative word is "give."

We've gotten a lot of I-feel-your-pain care lately, the mindless talk and cloying platitudes, the excuse-making b.s. It's high time for I Give A Damn (IGAD) care to have its day.

I Give A Damn is the thoughtful, courageous, active care at the core of democratic capitalism, and we are going to need every bit of IGAD if we are going to rescue capitalism from predatory collapse.

Without I Give A Damn care, functioning capitalism does not and cannot exist. The stalwarts of capitalism—value, productivity, quality, customer service, transparency, accountability, entrepreneurship, attention to detail, successful management, enforcement of law— all require that you give a damn.

IGAD doesn't require you to be liberal or conservative. In fact, it might help if you are neither. IGAD stands in sharp contrast to both unsustainable welfare state promises and corporate feudal monopolies currently masquerading as working in the people's interest.

*Democratic capitalism is about worthwhile production
and exchange by communities of people who give a damn.
It is expressly not about either crony-driven concentration
of wealth or government redistribution.*

IGAD doesn't accept fake "compassionate (neo-) conservatism" or fake "get-tough" liberalism. In fact, IGAD would prefer that both of these big-mouthed do-nothing ideologies and their champions shut up and get the bleep out of the way.

Since members of the status quo are clearly not going to step aside, it will be up to a fast-growing body of social, economic, cultural, political, educational, and spiritual independents to lead the charge through the status quo camp and beyond.

CONQUERING GREED AND SUPPORTING PRODUCTIVITY

Some people say that capitalism is built on greed or its euphemistic cousin "enlightened self-interest." It is not.

*Greed could be completely eliminated and democratic
capitalism would be all the better for it. Capitalism in the
absence of I Give A Damn, on the other hand,
would collapse immediately.*

Yes, Virginia, successful, healthy global economies are based on producing and giving something of value not on simply taking something of value. You wouldn't know this from the current climate of credit-crazed consumption and crony-driven market manipulation. Right now functioning capitalism is about as scarce as the real spirit of Christmas.

Greed has become a consuming wrecking crew, cannibalizing, exploiting, and appropriating assets, dumping liabilities on responsible citizens, and concentrating wealth in the top 0.1% in an unprecedented spectacle of what I call "financial obesity."

The economically starved productive class (the people who do actual work of value, i.e. middle and working classes) lies unaided and unseen behind the fat covering the eyes of the financial so-called "elite" (who should be called the financial "delete," because their only real talent seems to be in either stealing, wasting, or erasing value.)

This is what greed (and greed's crony, power) have brought us: a rising tide of debt and servitude built on exploitation and manipulation, quite the opposite of a rising tide of prosperity built on free enterprise promised by the so-called American Dream.

"But isn't greed human nature?" Greed is no more human nature than suicide is human nature. Right now, imbibing greed is suicide just as surely as drinking spiked kool-aid. I Give A Damn care, by contrast, is essential to any human nature that concerns itself with thriving and surviving in our new interdependent reality.

Supply is not the issue. There are plenty of people capable of giving a damn. Any time natural disasters strike, I Give A Damn citizens pour out of the woodwork.

Though currently submerged, I Give A Damn productivity needs to emerge and *start* winning the day. That requires choosing between the parts of our human nature—the desire to give and the desire to take—and then *deciding and following through* resolutely on the giving part. This means elevating our character, conviction, and good sense instead of cannibalizing each other.

Are we going to give a damn and contribute to new life or are we going to try to take down the world as we escape into death? Are we going to stand up, man up, and woman up, or leave our children and our planet with an irretrievable mess?

Without this decision foremost, all the technical talk and analysis about the economy is ultimately junk, the same junk composing junk bonds.

"Unite and Win": IGAD operational strategies

Since so much of the current global and national decision-making is being done by an exceedingly small band of incompetents and gluttons, we need not work to divide them. They are trying to divide us. We need to unite.

You give a damn, really? What have you been doing civically? Giving to Greenpeace or volunteering at the soup kitchen or attending Daughters of the American Revolution? Well, that's good start and we need it, but all the food pantries in the world won't make up for bad policies that eliminate food for hungry people!

Capitalist cronies will gladly take the surplus created by charity cost offloading to fund their military boondoggles and leave the middle and working classes both struggling on less and caring for the needy more. For any challenge to work, citizens need to get "systemic" and become smartly organized.

The time has never been riper to collaborate across the supposed dividing lines of ideologies. Haven't you been paying attention lately? Even Ronald Reagan's fiscal policy appointees Bruce "Supply-Side" Bartlett and David "Trickle Down" Stockman are sounding a regretful, almost progressive, tone. They now admit that their wealth-coddling ideology weakened conservatism and gave strength to party extremists.

Economic productivity and participation have plenty in common with traditional conservative values (self-reliance, fiscal responsibility, etc.) and traditional liberal values (concern for "least among us," etc.) not to mention activist, tech-savvy progressivism interested in creating sustainable ways to thrive.

The ad banner for unity should merely read: "Calling all sane, caring, inventive, substantive, hard-working people."

Qualifications:

1) Have your head upright, and not crammed into some orifice (yes, you Republicans who are not part of the bigoted nutjob segment of your party),

2) have some guts, (yes, you Democrats who remember what courage is and still utilize it), and

3) have an original, interdependent, creative, collaborative character.

Unity going forward does not require the *promise* of hope and change. Hope and change will be *realized* if we get down to business.

CITIZENS AS SAVVY POLITICAL ENTREPRENEURS

So-called "Powers That Be" assume organized citizens will fall for transparent co-optation. "What are your demands, Occupy Wall Street?", they say. Demands? How about just good-ole fashioned competition and pressure and relentless engagement. (Oh, pardon me... That wouldn't be fair. I forgot oligarchs no longer remember how to do competition with all their no-bid, insider contracts, and "cost-plus" accounting.)

I don't have to make demands as a citizen. I'm a leader. I get busy, I organize, I pressure, I create alternatives, and I keep working, working, and working until financial, political, and cultural exploiters fold.

> *There are no appeals to be made to a financial caste system that has proven it will not listen or change. Instead there is citizen conviction. There are reality-based principles and actions driven by the knowledge that the world can be a better place tomorrow if we use our minds, hearts, and efforts today.*

Be aware, idle rich: You are getting soft from the hypocrisy you keep slathering on your power lunches. We are not going to fall for promises, stop our activism, and then watch you fail to deliver yet again. (Obama, you'd better be listening, because you are and your sit-on-its-hands Justice Department are included.)

Nor are we going to watch you steal from us and then give us a cut of our own loot if we play ball. We are not going to agree to you borrowing from the future and piling debt on our kids.

> *Productive citizens don't have to make demands to financial freeloaders. We are the ones producing the value. We refuse to recognize your alleged authority. You have failed. We will develop and conduct our own leadership, value, and exchange.*

You, the idle rich, the financial delete, are expendable. You offer nothing, unless you are willing to roll up your sleeves and do some real work. So stop doing 'God's work' by stripping commissions from production, and start producing something of value. Be a stakeholder. Participate in the market. Be accountable to the market.

Be a democratic capitalist, for God's sake. That is our one and only requirement.

Confronting the false idols of corrupted capitalism

- **Having money never makes you better than someone else.** What is relevant is how you get your money. Any tool or crook can possess large sums of money.

- **Real personal worth involves human character and choices. It is not a financial dollar figure.** Without a sober assessment of human character and choices there is no way to make a distinction between producers and parasites, no social distinction between those who invest in constructive vs.

destructive enterprises. These distinctions are crucial in functioning capitalism.

- **Maximizing personal profit at any cost destroys capitalism and capitalist societies.** Additional financial profit can always be made by plundering natural resources and abusing people. That is not the kind of profit we can tolerate in democratic capitalism, even if it is available.

- **"Making money off the crisis" will drive capitalism into a sinkhole if it is dominated by profiteering from the misery of others, rather than from countering irrational exuberance.**

- **People who financially benefit from sucking, deceiving, lying, cheating, and stealing, should be thrown either into jail (fraudsters) or to the side of the road (talking heads, industry flacks, technocrats, etc.).**

If you make money by destroying people and their societies you are a corrupt capitalist, a looter, a thief, and and/or a murderer, period. If you are a government official who rewards these destruction-bringers, then both you and the private interests you prostitute yourself to must be defeated with democratic voting and citizen action.

Principled, effective actions for IGAD democratic capitalism

Revolutions start when growing groups of people congregate in cafes, taverns, meeting halls, and homes. For productive democratic capitalism to work, we need to get together and start doing the things that help our ability to survive and thrive, individually and collectively, and stop doing the things that harm.

- **Get your money out of too-big-too-fail banks, all of it.**
Move savings, money markets, retirement accounts. Divest
everything and both "strongly encourage" and help every
family member, neighbor, and investor to do the same. If Bank of
America can't respect the laws and principles of capitalism, then
maybe they will respect the laws of accounts: When you have
no money, you can't spend squat and you can't make a profit.
Welcome to what the rest of America is experiencing.

- **Rebel against the consumerist "American Dream" that
is making your life a nightmare.** If there is one thing you
should refuse to buy it's the media mantra that the solution
to everything is to just get consumer spending up, up, up. It's
a pyramid scheme run against a finite planet. This is a recipe
for destroying, not aiding, future generations. And spend with
what? Your great job that has not returned (or even materialized).
Your growing debt? Make reality your ally. Stop buying from
irresponsible corporations, buy second-hand goods from
friends and neighbors, and support community business with
the money you save.

- **Say "no" to debt servitude! If you cannot pay your
debt, seek legal, political, and personal solutions.**
Community-organize to provide low or no cost legal bankruptcy
protection. Work politically to get student loans to be discharge-
able debt. Research and get competent legal advice on how to
renounce or negotiate down debts to large companies you cannot
reasonably pay. "Moral sanctity of the contract" is demonstrated
by accepting the legal and financial consequences of failure. The
lendee loses equity and receives a bad credit rating for payment
failure. The lender receives financial loss for asset failure.

- **Say "yes" to strengthening, simplifying, and de-
expensing your life.** Take care of yourself physically,
mentally, emotionally, and spiritually. Don't eat garbage food.
Exercise regularly. Take non-essential activities and luxuries
(i.e. cable TV) off your plate. Attend a free book lecture. Donate
or sell the things you are not using. Meditate. Contemplate.

Vitalize. Organize. You are going to need every aspect of your health in peak condition to best meet and embrace the seismic world changes that will be coming much sooner than we all think.

- **Pool your money, resources, and time.** Even with their big infusions of taxpayer bailout money, banks aren't lending to Main Street. Do we really need them? Why not gather momentum around crowd-funding and circle lending at all levels. Why can't young people or young families move in together and share and trade their resources around childcare, meal preparation, elder care, professional skills and so forth. This mini "economies of scale" could free up significant space to develop an entrepreneurial business or spend more time organizing and developing the infrastructure for sustainable and fulfilling social and economic advancement.

CONCLUSION:

Corruption thrives when good people do nothing. Societies rebound when good people do something.

Let's do this. Let's make democratic capitalism happen.

11
YOUTH OF THE WORLD UNITE

*How Younger Generations Can Lead
the Way Toward a New Frontier*

Let's face it: The younger generations will be the ones paying for the sins and failures of previous generations. Those sins and failures are glaring. Yet, strangely, older generations appear intent on holding on to their power to make things even worse by doubling down on failed strategies while locking talented, resourceful, interconnected youth out of the process. This essay is an exhortation to give the emerging generations their due: If we collectively are going to stick youth with global society's problems, the least we can do is transfer power to them and acknowledge the necessity and centrality of their leadership. This essay points out how youth can initiate and create their own power and the rest of the world can help them.

INTRODUCTION

Older generations of the world have declared bankruptcy on their obligations to the young. They have turned in the keys and walked away from their social contract to make life better for succeeding generations. Conventional wisdom no longer provides credible answers to rising environmental abuse, opportunity impoverishment, or social disorder.

With few elder champions, world youth are forced to respond. This article hopes to aid an effective response by laying out the current global challenges for youth, presenting effective remedies, and offering future possible directions.

In crucial times of change it is for the young to lead, to transform willful ignorance, entitlement, and self-absorption into wisdom, service, and collaboration, to solve complex problems and generate a new quality of life.

The current challenges: Youth, debt, and a global crisis of opportunity

Lying to ourselves will serve no one. The first step in organizing an effective response to the world is to provide a "myth-free zone". Here are the common key issues and uncomfortable realities confronting young people around the world today:

1) Debt servitude
2) Unemployment
3) Diminished opportunity for talent development, leadership, and contribution
4) Silenced voices: Generational inequality and lack of representation
5) Disappearing meritocracy

Debt servitude

Unserviceable debt creates an endless trap. In the U.S. where student loan debt cannot be erased in bankruptcy, this can mean a lifetime of indentured servitude. Combined with unemployment, it robs the debt-afflicted of meaning, worth, and self-determination, a basic human requirement. With soaring college tuition costs and sharply contracting job markets, youth are particularly hit by this phenomenon.

On the April 27th 2012 episode of "On the Edge" I talked with Max Keiser about the "debt plague" infecting youth (http://www.youtube.com/watch?v=FxSApTlPmhE#t=6m27s):

> **Max:** "You often talk about the fraudulent nature of debt. In America, student loan debts have surpassed total outstanding credit card debt. More than 25% of that is delinquent. Is this a sign of predation, debt-plagueness?"

Zeus: "It is... and indentured servitude as well. You don't get those kinds of numbers without predatory lending, or extremely unwise lending, or both. All this was premised upon easy supply of money, which drove the cost of education sky high, way, way above the price of inflation. So you have predation and a con game that you would get these massively high paid, high skill jobs, once you got your college degree. Well, that hasn't panned out. In fact, the economy is adding low skill, low pay jobs at a much, much higher rate."

"Students are caught in a bind. They simply cannot pay their student loans, and there is no foreseeable future in which they will get the kinds of jobs they need to pay (them)... We're going to have to have a democratic response. It just isn't sustainable."

I went on to call out the socially criminal nature of excluding student loans from bankruptcy. If something is found to be worthless in the market, it deserves to be marked down to zero.

Unemployment

Unemployment adds to the crushing weight of debt servitude, and further invites serious social consequences. Unemployment among youth is spiking up around the globe and has reached over 50% in Spain and Greece (http://www.thedailybeast.com/newsweek/2012/07/15/are-millennials-the-screwed-generation.html).

Those consequences are already severe, concrete, and present, not simply future. Chase Cryn Johansen details in her Huffington Post piece the hopelessness and impacts on suicide rates that debt servitude and unemployment can cause. (http://www.huffingtonpost.com/c-cryn-johannsen/student-loan-debt-suicides_b_1638972.html#es_share_ended)

Diminished opportunity for talent development, leadership, and contribution

Rising debt and vanishing work may remain the central practical economic challenges for emerging generations, but these are far from the only challenges confronting youth. Culturally supported personal growth, civic leadership, and career advancement, have also largely been shelved in the rush to prop up the fortunes of older generations.

Youthful talent is being exploited rather than developed. Youth leadership is being squandered rather than mentored. Uncorrected, these generational trends invite social rupture—discontinuity, disaffection, and alienation between generations.

> (S)ome of the most talented people here in the workforce in the Philippines (and around the world) are the people in their 20's and 30's. They are the ones passing the civil service exams, and they are the ones able to use the technology to help (their) country advance. But (young people who are talented and should rise) are just not given the leadership or the power. Older people are holding on to the levers of power, and they are not turning them over... If you really want to turn the global economy around, and get Asian economies working, you are not simply going to honor the older generations, but you are going to open opportunities to the younger generations. I don't see that happening really globally anywhere." (Zeus Yiamouyiannis on Max Keiser's "On the Edge," April 27, 2012 http://www.youtube.com/watch?v=Fx-SApTlPmhE#t=8m16s)

Silenced voices: Generational inequality and lack of representation

After being key to Barack Obama's electoral success in 2008, volunteering, organizing, and voting in large numbers, young Americans found themselves quickly on the outside. After being told they would be needed even more once Obama gained office, their concerns, their needs, and their emails were promptly swept into a closet and forgotten.

A few token nods to reinvigorating a Franklin Delano Roosevelt style volunteer corps and paying off student loans with pro-social work, substituted for concrete actual change. Headed into an uninspiring 2012, younger generations knew that the reality with Mitt Romney's political party would be significantly worse: anti-immigrant, anti-gay, anti-minority bigotry mixed with a blind anti-tax ideology that requires borrowing even more from future generations to fund burgeoning entitlement payments now.

Even labor unions appear to have reversed the whole notion of a "union" by negotiating lower pay and benefits for younger members to retain the higher pay and benefits for older members. (http://www.npr.org/2012/04/04/149991140/italian-law-pits-older-workers-against-younger-ones)(http://corymccray.com/2011/05/tier-systems-cripple-middle-class-dreams-for-young-workers/)

This is hardly "change you can believe in." Very few champions or mentors for younger citizens have stepped forward. Far more people have used young citizens as exploitable fodder for their own advancement and profit. Young people are beginning to recognize that they will have to embody Gandhi's paraphrased sentiment, "Be the change that you wish to see in the world."

Disappearing meritocracy

Much ado has been made about younger generations' impatience with "working their way up from the bottom." In some quarters this complaint is justified, but in just as many situations young people have a coherent response: "If I can do it better, why do I have to wait my turn?" What ought to be the higher principle, seniority or efficacy? Why are twenty-something's only rewarded (sometimes with billions) in internet and tech start-ups?

Perhaps more credence could be given the ability of younger generations to share and prove their ability in an environment of patient mentorship. Raw ability could be integrated more smoothly into institutional cultures.

Capitalist markets supposedly reward greater adaptability, effectiveness, and efficiency. Cultural conventions protect against change that is too rapid by elevating age and tenure. Yet most changes now are happening very quickly. The best of the past should be married with the best of the present and future.

FIGHTING BACK: CREATING A BASIS FOR GENERATIONAL SUPPORT

Skyrocketing debt and unemployment among global youth bring into view a more foundational life issue: How can young people not only earn a living and develop effective service, but gain autonomy, empowerment, and quality of life? How might youth organize and re-create themselves through their own initiative and choices regardless of how much (or little) opportunity they are offered by others?

EMPOWERING THE FUTURE: TRANSFORMING CHALLENGES INTO CREATIVE PRACTICES

The big secret is this: When it comes to proactive citizen involvement we don't have to wait for permission. When a generational social contract is broken, grievance and appeal are unlikely to yield results. So, an opportunity emerges to put our energy into developing our own resources, leadership, and networks, and recruit allies for that purpose.

Yes, captured law, skewed priorities, and weak character have resulted in an unsustainable global pyramid scheme around work and resources. Yes, many people have defaulted on their obligations to provide for a healthy, sustainable future. Now it is our obligation is to develop the viable alternatives.

Arab Spring was driven largely by educated youth without jobs. Occupy Wall Street had a very similar profile. Both are having trouble making the transition from an effective resistance force to a cohesive proactive force. Younger generations already know that being co-opted doesn't work. They refuse to be bought off and brought back into unsustainable schemes, but what is the alternative?

As described in the above sections, the first step is recognizing what is going on. The second step is exercising effective civil disobedience and severing exploitation through collective and personal choices and actions. The third step involves the more demanding and more complex task of creating a new future.

What might be some of the pillars of this new generational way?

1) **Non-material value over material value:** There is a quiet revolution in value going on. This goes far beyond the demand for free ware and open source software. Poll after poll is showing that once a living wage and basic benefits are attained at work, younger generation prefer productive, pleasant teamwork and opportunity for meaningful professional and pro-social development over salary. (http://www. forbes.com/sites/mattmiller/2012/07/03/why-you-should-be-hiring-millennials-infographic/). This trend will hopefully gain strength and speed.

As I noted in a discussion group on alternative futures:

(T)he most important things in life" (love, community, diversity, etc.) are all non-material, and we are using consumption, material resources, and products as... proxies for these most important things. Non-material "goods" have the advantage of being non-scarce, unlimited in supply (if handled correctly and not oppressed by material concerns), and increasing (rather than decreasing) in value the more they are shared. We [as a whole] simply aren't yet committed to pursuing what is most important, of highest quality. Until the exercise of spirit and creative productivity are seen as the core rather than an idle luxury we will be fighting over dwindling resources." (https://www.yammer.com/atca/#/threads/show?threadId=189655364&messageId=190335467)

It looks like younger generations will be leading the way in this effort.

2) **Collaborative employment:** If the point of work is to simply receive a living wage and to maximize non-material benefits, then it would make sense to "spread the employment wealth" rather than to simply compete for a greater share of the pie (in personal salary, celebrity, and authority). This would create jobs and jobs with a very different function. Project-based work could increasingly become collective efforts requiring greater application of individual talent and new tools for future development.

3) **Renewed voice: True representation and social media:** Why not have a World Youth Congress nominated and elected through social media? Members of the younger generation could be elected to represent the interests of their generation. Expertise and authority would rest in the ability of representatives to listen, organize, focus, and collaborate in such a way as to send a loud message through collective actions. This could include boycotting destructive corporations, abandoning sell-out political candidates, supporting crowd funding for needed innovations, or even creating artistic events meant to inspire, equip, and entertain.

Why not create a social media news service that reflects the challenges, needs, and concerns of younger generations instead of misrepresenting and insulting those concerns?

4) **Networked, resource-minded leadership, creativity, and entrepreneurialism:** This requires a move from "Why me?" to "Why not us?" When no one is willing to invest in you, perhaps the best solution is to find ways to co-invest with others in living arrangements, in job hiring, in crowd funding, in the way one volunteers time, focus, and intention.

No terrain should go unexplored. If college is too expensive, if it is dispensing out-of-touch education, and is not producing promised job results, why not organize around creating free, high-quality, relevant higher education. There is nothing stopping youth from researching accreditation and strategically drawing upon source and online learning to develop demonstrated competencies that nail current ability measures, end-run monopolistic gatekeepers, and apply useful ideas.

5) **Meritocracy 2.0:** Young people have the ultimate meritocratic challenge. They have to create a sustainable, fulfilling world. Fail in that, and it won't matter how highly they have been promoted up their respected job ladders. Social problem-solving and effectiveness have to gain precedence over hype or seniority.

This is already beginning in an organic, unrecognized global youth revolt, combining Eastern and Western traits: humility and conviction, attention to detail and creativity, mindfulness and achievement. The "de-Generation" in Japan, for instance, is experimenting with extremely resourceful, earth and technologically-connected living (http://www.youtube.com/watch?v=y395J6W6i1E).

CHALLENGES AND QUESTIONS

The challenges and questions are clear. The possible answers and paths forward are fuzzy. Few in history are so lucky to live in an era requiring such fertile imagination, intense focus, and human effort. But this is the moment that embraced life prepares us for and provides for us. It is up to us to find a way to respond with gratitude and vigor.

Our map is before us. We are moving from "New Era" thinking based upon delusionary premises of ever-expanding material growth, toward one of "Vital Future" where material is conserved and respected as a way to support the creation and evolution of non-material goods and growth.

Old "New Era" thinking:

1) Value of assets only goes up.

2) Wealth expansion is infinite and need not be limited by material assets and what people can pay for things.

3) Having relatively more of a "good thing" dilutes its worth and lowers its value. The scarcer a "good thing" is, the more it gains value.

4) People who share a material product are losers who can't buy it for themselves.

5) It's all a zero-sum, competitive, dog-eat-dog game out there, but somehow everyone can be rich.

6) Everyone is entitled to, and ought to desire, easy, comfortable, individual living.

7) The good life is one of exploiting and consuming.

8) It's most important to look out for number one.

9) Democracy is for suckers. It's a game you play to make everyone think they are participating and benefiting equally. The real money is in using the idea of democracy married with dreams of riches to get everyone addicted to debt.

New "Vital Future" thinking:

1) Physical assets and their value are limited. The most abundant and fulfilling elements of life are non-material in nature (love, community, creativity, awareness, etc.) and unlimited.

2) Since non-material elements are infinite, they can be produced without practical limit.

3) The value of these non-material "good things," *increases and multiplies,* rather than diminishes, the more they are shared and the more they are present.

4) There is only win-win, where material and non-material assets are responsibly shared and exchanged, and lose-lose, when assets are not shared and exchanged.

5) The best social organization is neither collectivism nor individualism, but an interaction between the two: "I am a more fulfilled 'me,' by a more effective 'we'."

6) Anyone leading an honest, open life will be challenged and surprised into contributing something unique.

7) The good life is one of creating, producing, and sharing.

8) It's most important to serve others, especially the next generations.

9) Grass-roots democracy and locally-driven, globally-aware coordinated action will be the primary avenue out of this mess.

CONCLUSION

Value Lives and Rests With Us

I n the introduction to this book, I made the critical distinction between measuring value and having value. Money has no worth. It merely measures worth. Money represents value, or in the case of modern economy, represents pseudo-value. But where does value itself reside? Where is the substance of value?

Value lives and rests with us— our choices, our productivity, our care, our creativity, our love for one another, our subjectivity. There is no object with inherent value, but the value we confer to it with our human desire. Gold means nothing. Diamonds mean nothing. They are shiny, durable symbols of shared desire for beauty and immortality.

That is why we agree to let them to cost so much money. Their physical properties are convincing proxies for the real thing. Gold retains its luster and radiance better than other metals. Diamonds aren't "forever" but last nearly so, as far as we are concerned.

If this book has communicated one insight, I hope it is this: The "good life" is not based on symbols or proxies or objects or other middlemen to joy. It is based directly in deep experience and deep connection. The highest human activities do this the best—creating, giving, producing, sharing. The lowest human activities do this the worst— destroying, taking, exploiting, abusing.

It makes no sense to assign blame and simply react to the evils of the world or to run like a survivalist into the woods. The cure to the disease is a daring but thrilling one: Unchain ourselves from symbols and agents and vicarious experience, and accept the responsibility to live a life of deep regard, meaning, and respect *now*. In doing so, we lead a life worth living *for,* and we leave an earth worth living *on* for future generations.

May we follow the simple words of the great mystic Hillel:

> Love your neighbor as yourself. All the rest is commentary. Now go and learn."

Bless the journey,

Zeus Yiamouyiannis

Further Reading and Viewing

Recommended economics blogs:

http://www.oftwominds.com/blog.html (Charles Hugh Smith)
http://www.peakprosperity.com/ (Chris Martenson)
http://theautomaticearth.com/ (The Automatic Earth)
http://maxkeiser.com/ (Max Keiser)
http://www.debtdeflation.com/blogs/ (Steve Keen)
http://www.ritholtz.com/blog/ (Barry Ritholtz)
http://globaleconomicanalysis.blogspot.com/ (Mike Shedlock)
http://www.zerohedge.com/ (Various contributors)
http://seekingalpha.com/ (Various contributors)
http://www.boombustblog.com/ (Reggie Middleton)
http://www.itulip.com/ (Eric Janszen)

Recommended books:

Why the World is Falling Apart and What We Can Do About It
(by Charles Hugh Smith, http://www.oftwominds.com/CHS-books.html)

Survival +: Structuring Prosperity for Yourself and the Nation
(by Charles Hugh Smith, http://www.oftwominds.com/CHS-books.html)

The Truth in Money Book
(by Theodore R. Thoren and Richard E. Warner, http://www.amazon.com/Truth-Money-book-Theodore-Thoren/dp/0960693815)

The Future of Money
(by Bernard Lietaer, http://www.lietaer.com/writings/books/the-future-of-money/)

Recommended videos:

Zeus Yiamouyiannis on Debt Forgiveness, Keiser Report:
(http://www.youtube.com/watch?v=MGmayjYQpB8#t=13m2s)

Zeus Yiamouyiannis on Greek Economic Tragedies and Greek
Solutions, Keiser Report:
(http://www.youtube.com/watch?v=J3Ex4okWm-M#t=12m36s)

Zeus Yiamouyiannis on the European Sovereign and Debt Crisis
and Asian Economies, On the Edge with Max Keiser:
(http://www.youtube.com/watch?v=FxSApTlPmhE#t=0m25s)

Zeus Yiamouyiannis on Shadow Banking, Inside the Eye:
(https://www.youtube.com/watch?v=qu2JZ1B005g)

About the Author

Zeus Yiamouyiannis, Ph.D. is an economics blogger, futurist, and author of *Transforming Economy: From Corrupted Capitalism to Connected Communities*. He has written regularly for top alternative economics blogs, including OfTwoMinds.com and ZeroHedge.com. He has appeared as a guest on "The Keiser Report" and "On the Edge with Max Keiser" on RT TV as well as the "Inside the Eye" radio program. Zeus is a "performance educator" with expertise in philosophy and cultural foundations of education. His own blog, Citizen Zeus, focuses on "learning to transform," especially in the areas of economics, education, and spirituality. This background, combined with economics understanding, yields an incisive, comprehensive analysis. Zeus applies his original, integrated perspective in *Transforming Economy* so readers can anticipate emerging economic trends and creatively respond.

BUY NOW

  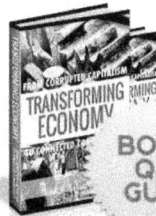

$ 14.95

NOW $9.95

JUST ONE PLEASE

$ 19.95

NOW $14.95

FRIENDS AND FAMILY SHARE
LESS THAN $3.75 PER BOOK

$ 34.95

NOW $24.95

SPECIAL DISCUSSION GROUP RATE
LESS THAN $2.30 PER BOOK

TRANSFORMINGECONOMY.COM/GET-THE-BOOK

www.ingramcontent.com/pod-product-compliance
Lightning Source LLC
Chambersburg PA
CBHW071637200326
41519CB00012BA/2332